JUDSON PRESS

PUBLISHERS SINCE 1824

Advance Praise for Marriage ROCKS

"This **wonderful book** serves a need in the African American community for help in **strengthening and healing our marriages** and relationships. The author provides honest examples that will be a blessing to those who are considering marriage and those who are already on the journey. The message is clear—whether your marriage is strong already or deeply troubled, God can make it better and help you deepen spiritual and emotional intimacy."

—Nancy Boyd-Franklin, PhD, author of *Black Families in Therapy: Understanding the African American Experience*

"Married couples are on the endangered species list. Dr. Harold Arnold's **expertise and passion** are focused on preserving and strengthening African American marriages. His years of helping couples is reflected in this powerful *Marriage ROCKS* 'journey,' which has couples interacting and praying about topics that will enrich their personal and intimate lives together. But it's not just about you! He goes on to teach and challenge couples how to use their marriages as a **powerful tool for sharing Christ** with all who live in their communities. Every couple who wants to grow in their relationship with each other and with Christ will benefit from this interactive marriage experience."

—Bruce R. McCracken, PhD, founder and president, House on the Rock Family Ministries

"At a time when the institution of marriage seems under attack, *Marriage ROCKS* provides a **refreshing and affirming view of marriage.** Dr. Arnold's five components of ROCKS are grounded in sound biblical principles and relational integrity."

—Randolph Walters, PsyD, marriage therapist and associate professor of counseling psychology, Eastern University

"What a tribute *Marriage ROCKS for Christian Couples* is to the field of marriage enrichment. This resource is a real gem for couples and leaders who care about strengthening and deepening marriage vows. **Grounded in biblical truths** and psychological sensitivity, this book offers a treasure trove of ways to build on God as the Rock, the faithful One who provides shelter and hope in the storms and serenities of marital life."

—Judith Balwick, EdD, senior professor of marital and family therapy, Fuller Theological Seminary

"AMEN! Harold Arnold boldly imparts the ageless principles, **fresh insights, and practical skills** that can and will revitalize African American marriages in the home . . . and the black community. While aimed at African American relationships, *Marriage ROCKS* has something for all couples, 'red, brown, yellow, black, or white.' This white guy from the Northwest is standing up in the pew shouting, 'Preach it!'"

—K. Jason Krafsky, author of *Before "I Do":*
Preparing for the Full Marriage Experience

"The illusions created by Hollywood and the booming romance industry are destroying today's marriages, causing divorce rates to climb higher than they have in years. *Marriage ROCKS* has all the tools we need to start picking up the pieces and getting our relationships back in line with those **values that are important to all Christians.** The thing I like most about *Marriage ROCKS* is that it provides **practical, reader-friendly tools** and lessons not only on *what* to do, but *how* to do it."

—Elder Rob Harrison, MA, founder and president,
4EverMarriages & Families

MARRIAGE ROCKS

for christian couples

HAROLD L. ARNOLD JR., PhD

JUDSON PRESS

PUBLISHERS SINCE 1824

VALLEY FORGE, PA

Marriage ROCKS for Christian Couples

© 2009 by Harold L. Arnold Jr.

All rights reserved.

Published in association with the Books & Such Literary Agency, 52 Mission Circle, Suite 122, PMB 170, Santa Rosa, CA 95409-5370, www.booksandsuch.biz.

Judson Press and the author have made every effort to trace the ownership of all quotes. In the event of a question arising from the use of a quote, we regret any error made and will be pleased to make the necessary correction in future printings and editions of this book.

Bible quotations in this volume are taken from the *Holy Bible, New International Version®. NIV®.* Copyright © 1973, 1978, 1984 by International Bible Society. Used by permission of Zondervan. All rights reserved; and from New Revised Standard Version Bible, copyright 1989, Division of Christian Education of the National Council of the Churches of Christ in the United States of America. Used by permission. All rights reserved.

Library of Congress Cataloging-in-Publication Data
Arnold, Harold L.
    Marriage ROCKS for Christian couples / Harold L. Arnold, Jr. — 1st ed.
        p.   cm.
    Includes bibliographical references (p.   ).
    ISBN 978-0-8170-1566-4 (pbk. : alk. paper) 1. Spouses—Religious life—Textbooks. 2. African Americans—Religious life—Textbooks. 3. Marriage—Religious aspects—Christianity—Textbooks. I. Title.

BR563.N4.A758   2009
248.8'4408996073—dc22

                                                                2009040072

Printed in the U.S.A.
First Edition, 2009.

Contents

Foreword

Oliver Thomas wrote in the September 14, 2009, edition of *USA Today* an article entitled "Is Secularism Saving Marriage?" The point of the article was that people are discovering on their own, without the aid of the church, the truth about why marriage works. Couples are learning that intimacy, mutuality, and gender equality are what make marriage effective. The article is critical of some church leaders because they refuse to allow women to share authority in the family. The article concludes that wider culture understands that gender equality is the chief characteristic that makes marriage work, whereas some religious leaders continue to promote male-dominated patriarchy within the marriage.

In contrast, Harold L. Arnold Jr., PhD, has written a book for African American couples rooted thoroughly in a faith orientation, and it draws on a biblical and theological tradition of gender mutuality and equality that is embraced by many African American couples. My wife and I have been doing marital enrichment workshops with African American Christians since the mid 1980s, and it is clear to us that couples desire to build their marriages on a strong biblical foundation. Moreover, African American women expect their men to be responsible participants and leaders in the family while at the same time practicing genuine intimacy, mutuality, and equality in gender relationships. Arnold's book, *Marriage ROCKS for Christian Couples*, recognizes and responds to these real and felt needs—to have marriages grounded biblically and theologically while drawing on scriptural principles of gender equality and mutuality.

Arnold is more than capable of addressing the felt need of African American Christian couples. He earned his PhD in social and organizational psychology from Temple University, and he holds a master's degree in marriage and family therapy from Fuller

Theological Seminary. In addition, his approach to marital enrichment draws from the behavioral and social science counseling psychologies those principles that correspond well with biblical and theological values. He demonstrates an ability to use these secular disciplines of marriage and family therapy toward Christian growth and formation ends. In other words, for him there is no antagonism between biblical and theological marital and family values and the theories of marriage and family life drawn from contemporary behavioral and social sciences.

There are several significant dimensions of the book that need to be highlighted. I have already lifted up the relevance of biblical and theological ideas to contemporary marital enrichment. In addition, this book is a competent practical guide for African Americans and for couples of different cultural backgrounds who are nervous about engaging in the process of marital enrichment. More precisely, the approach will enable men from any ethnic origin to engage in the process without fear. The book also implicitly lifts up the sacramental potential of marriage in the sense that marriage is truly a means of conveying God's grace to others. Finally, the book is a reliable practical guide that is not only Christian in orientation; it also utilizes the best practices and discoveries of contemporary martial and family disciplines to help couples.

I commend this book because it delivers what it set out to deliver. It provides what it promises it will from the outset, and those who use this book as a resource for marital enrichment will never regret their choice.

Edward P. Wimberly, PhD
Jarena Lee Professor of Pastoral Care and Counseling
Vice President for Academic Affairs/Provost
Interdenominational Theological Center
Atlanta, Georgia

Acknowledgments

Unbeknown to me for many years is the simple fact that the positive and challenging aspects of the marriages around me have had an impact on my life from childhood to adulthood. Like stones that are shaped by years of exposure to nature's elements, *Marriage ROCKS* has been forming in my life for a long time.

First, I wish to honor my maternal grandmother, Minnie H. Penn, who helped me as a child to maintain a positive image of marriage in the midst of difficult circumstances. Before her death my grandmother commissioned Dalia and me to use our lives to impact marriages. *Marriage ROCKS* is a fulfillment of her prophetic voice.

I am grateful to my parents, Rev. Harold L. Arnold Sr. and Dorothy Arnold, for providing a living example that marriage is for a lifetime, even when conflict is present. Your journey has been my journey. I love you both. *Marriage ROCKS* is a testimony to your perseverance.

I am indebted to my children, Quilan and Kyrsten, for being willing to give up time with me as I pursue my writing career. Your amazing lives reinforce the importance of why healthy marriages benefit the children most.

I wish to thank my wife, Dalia. Throughout the writing of the book, you have been a nurturer. You are the keeper of my dreams. Every chapter of this book reflects the hopes that I have for our marriage. And in many ways, I believe that *Marriage ROCKS* is the vision God has given us to make an impact on the world with the love that we have shared for two decades.

Finally, to my friend Joanne Weidman, thank you for your countless hours of allowing God to use your editing gifts and clinical excellence to shape what *Marriage ROCKS* has become. Your words of encouragement and insight have been a constant source of strength.

PART ONE

The Case for Authentic Marriage

BIBLICAL VIGNETTE:
The Creation of Marriage

The LORD God said, "It is not good for the man to be alone. I will make a helper suitable for him." Now the LORD God had formed out of the ground all the beasts of the field and all the birds of the air. He brought them to the man to see what he would name them; and whatever the man called each living creature, that was its name. So the man gave names to all the livestock, the birds of the air and all the beasts of the field. But for Adam no suitable helper was found. So the LORD God caused the man to fall into a deep sleep; and while he was sleeping, he took one of the man's ribs and closed up the place with flesh. Then the LORD God made a woman from the rib he had taken out of the man, and he brought her to the man. The man said, "This is now bone of my bones and flesh of my flesh; she shall be called 'woman,' for she was taken out of man." For this reason a man will leave his father and mother and be united to his wife, and they will become one flesh. The man and his wife were both naked, and they felt no shame. (Genesis 2:18-25, NIV)

CHAPTER 1

Marriage Is for God's People

The Christian ideal has not been
tried and found wanting.
It has been found difficult;
and left untried.
—G.K. CHESTERTON

You deserve more from your marriage! Without even knowing you or the details of your marriage, I declare this boldly. Are you nodding your head in enthusiastic agreement, since you have been getting the short end of the stick in your relationship? Are you wondering what I mean, because things are going well for you? Perhaps you disagree with me, because you are getting just what you deserve (and maybe more) because of the mistakes you have made. Nevertheless, I am sticking to my assertion—though I may need to convince you of my logic.

Here is my thinking: You are a child of God. Just as those of you who are parents desire the best for your children, so God desires the best for his. If you are reading this book, it is because you desire the best for your marriage. You can rest assured that God desires the best for your marriage as well. Marriage is not for everyone, but you have chosen to enter into that covenant, and God honors this choice. In fact, God plans to use your marriage as a bridge to a more rewarding relationship with him and with everyone within your sphere of influence over the course of your life (believe it or not).

Think about famous bridges: San Francisco's Golden Gate, Manhattan's Brooklyn, England's Humber, or Japan's Akashi-Kaikyo. These amazing spans are not famous for their functional utility but rather for their stellar engineering and architecture.

These technological marvels attract admiration and praise to the cities where they exist and to the people who created them.

In the mind of God, your marriage was created as a beautiful display of God's genius. It too is intended to direct the praise and admiration of everyone to its creator, God. I say again: Your marriage is a bridge to God. God desires you to have your best marriage, because your marvelous marriage will connect you, your family, and your community to him like no other human relationship. You deserve more in your marriage because your marriage has yet to achieve the level of beauty and influence that God has in mind for you. You deserve more in your marriage because God promises in his Word that he will perform abundantly more in your life than you can ask or imagine (Ephesians 3:20). You deserve more in your marriage because there is untapped potential within you that God wants to unleash.

Why marriage? I am convinced that it is the most tangible and important tool for personal, familial, and communal growth. Yet, an increasing number of single and married persons alike are struggling with the question, why marriage? Although for many generations, such a question may have been considered silly, today, even African Americans of faith seem to waver.

Younger generations like the freedom and flexibility of having sex, living together, and even having children before marriage, with fewer perceived obligations. Not long ago I was stunned to hear an inner-city African American youth saying, "Marriage is for white people." Although initially I had hoped this sentiment was isolated to small enclaves, the broader truth appears starker. African American youths are not quoting U.S. Census data on marriage; they are simply communicating that their experience has been devoid of two-parent households, much less married parents. Absent personal experience, their views of marriage are detached from reality, informed by fictitious portrayals on television or other media outlets.

The question of why marriage, however, is not limited to younger generations. Older people, often themselves products of single-parent homes, may not see marriage as a realistic option either. Still others who did enter holy matrimony feel cheated by marriages that have failed to live up to their lofty expectations. For many African Americans, marriage simply feels irrelevant or, worse, impractical.

Evidence suggests that marriage may be losing to more secular values. African Americans have one of the lowest marriage rates in the country, and our divorce rate is among the highest. So, why marriage? Reflect on your own ideas about what marriage means to you. How much of your answer is about a personal quest for physical, spiritual, and emotional satisfaction? If you think marriage is *only* about your personal fulfillment, then I am grateful that you are seeking a more comprehensive perspective. On the other hand, if your marital expectations do not include personal fulfillment, this book also offers hope for you. This hope is that marriage is indeed for white people and is equally relevant for the African American culture and for every other ethnic group. Further, while secular-minded individuals grapple with the relevance of the institution of marriage, the Holy Scripture teaches us that marriage is for God's people. This does not mean that, in order to be godly, you must desire marriage, nor does it suggest that non-Christians do not value marriage. It means that God designed marriage as a covenant relationship modeled after his relationship with those who worship him.

> God designed marriage as a covenant
> relationship modeled after his relationship
> with those who worship him.

Now that you have thought about what marriage means for you, ask yourself a second question: Does your answer capture what God intends for your marriage? For many, the answer would be no, because our understanding of marriage is limited. The belief that marriage is just for white people is not just a flaw in the thinking of one or two African American youths; it is an indictment of the African American community. While there are sociological explanations (e.g., slavery's devaluation of the family unit) as to why many of our African American youth have such a distorted perspective, this is not our focus here. Rather, our task is to remedy African Americans' intimate relationships, so that they may become beacons of light for individuals, families, and the broader African American community.

The word *community* is important. Thinking again of the young African American man's perception of marriage, a community phenomenon fuels his errant thinking. Not surprisingly, it will be a community response that provides correction. I am encouraged by the efforts of organizations such as The Wedded Bliss Foundation, which has instituted a national Black Marriage Day to celebrate black marriage.[1] Communities from around the nation come together to collectively renew our commitment to the institution of marriage.

Marriage ROCKS: A Community Model

Marriage ROCKS offers another model that facilitates this community response. In this regard, you are encouraged to discuss this book with a small group of other couples—engaged or married. Each chapter includes a series of personal reflections as well as couple exercises to encourage dialogue. The *Marriage ROCKS* Leader's Guide also includes activities and discussion questions to encourage group dialogue and interaction. After incorporating these *Marriage ROCKS* principles into your marriage, I am confident that your convictions about your own marriage (or marriage to be) and the marriages of those in your circle of influence will be forever changed.

I hope you are excited that you are only steps away from understanding how God answers the question, why marriage? Through this book and your small group experience, my charge to you is to discover God's mind. If that feels impossible based on your own struggles with the marriage question, let me assure you that the journey has already begun. As you experience the *Marriage ROCKS* program, you will unearth a treasure—a married life built upon authentic meaning—a treasure that taps into our most intimate needs for both purpose and companionship. *Marriage ROCKS* challenges the human tendency to become complacent with the status quo in our intimate relationships, suggesting that

God desires to activate your marriage beyond what you imagined possible. As you allow God to speak new life, you will receive a priceless return on your investment. I am excited that you have started the journey.

The Marriage ROCKS Method

First, let me be clear. There is nothing uniquely African American about the *Marriage ROCKS* method itself. It can be tailored through small-group dialogue and activities to transform intimate relationships across cultural landscapes. However, it has been designed in a delivery format and with themes that are sensitive to the struggles of African American relationships. In other words, this book is deliberately tailored to an African American perspective.

The *Marriage ROCKS* method is interwoven with the religious cord that runs through the African American community. Recent research by the Pew Research Center highlights the importance of religion in black America, with 85 percent of church-attending African Americans reporting that religion serves a very important role in their lives—a figure higher than all other American ethnic groups.[2] Another study concludes that African Americans are more likely than whites, Hispanics, and Asians to have religious beliefs that "parallel Christian or biblical teachings."[3] This research shows African Americans are more likely to believe that the Bible is accurate in what it teaches and that religious faith is very important in their lives. The role of the African American church since the days of slavery is well documented. For hundreds of years, the African American community has looked to religion and biblically based solutions for guidance in surviving and thriving through the most difficult of circumstances. *Marriage ROCKS* builds upon this desire for God-centered, biblical authenticity to promote a perspective on marriage that will enable us to thrive as an African American community.

Every book, program, and seminar on marriage, whether religious or secular, takes a perspective on marriage problems and solutions. Proposed solutions always depend upon the lens through which the problem is understood. *Marriage ROCKS* is designed to align with God's Word by invoking biblical principles, vignettes, and characters to inform your understanding of marriage, so Scripture is the lens of *Marriage ROCKS*.

Although the *Marriage ROCKS* principles are set in a scriptural context, each of the five components is fundamental to Christians and non-Christians alike. In fact, if you can recruit some non-Christians into your small-group discussions, I am confident that you and they will see the principles as equally relevant. If you have been looking for an evangelistic outreach or mentoring relationship with other couples, *Marriage ROCKS* is for you, too.

Ultimately, *Marriage ROCKS* challenges you to recognize that neither your life nor your marriage belongs to you. It has been purchased for a price (1 Corinthians 7:23), Christ's death on Calvary's cross. As such, your marriage is a ministry. Your marriage can and should be an outreach, drawing your neighbors to the light of Christ.

Why do I use the metaphor of rocks? The Bible offers many illustrations using rocks. David uses compelling imagery in Psalm 61, borrowed from the Torah, of God as the Rock. Deuteronomy 32 describes God as both the rock of salvation (32:15) and the rock that begat Israel (32:18). Rock is a symbol of permanence and strength against a myriad of pressures. The rock is a fortress of protection from the storms of life. As we work to align our African American marriages with God's lens, we must stand on God, the Solid Rock, as the source of our strength. Where do you go when the storms of life are threatening your marriage?

Satan would have you believe that all of the answers to your marriage lie within you. This is not true. In reality, the answers lie in God. The will to reach for those answers lies in you.

The *Marriage ROCKS* method suggests that your desperation must bring you to the end of yourself and to the beginning of God. God promises to take ownership of the storms when we lean on him. God promises to be our shelter, because the battles that we fight are not ours but his (2 Chronicles 20:15). God is, therefore, the focus of *Marriage ROCKS*. Satan, the enemy of marriage, would have you believe that all of the answers to your marriage lie within you. This is not true. In reality, the answers lie in God. The will to reach for those answers lies in you. Submit your marriage to God, your Rock, for his divine management. The permanence and strength that you desire for your African American marriage can only be found in the Rock.

Maximizing Your Marriage ROCKS Experience

The remainder of this book is designed to foster an intimate familiarity with the five rocks of authentic marriage, by taking your marriage on a twelve-step journey of discovery. Each rock is presented within the context of a biblical vignette, in which geological rocks are a central object of focus and learning for four biblical heroes of the faith: David, Gideon, Jacob, and Joshua. We earlier discussed the pervasive use of rocks in the Scripture to communicate faith lessons to God's people. This was likely because of the presence of rocks as a natural resource in the land of Israel. God continues to use these rocks as symbols for his people today.

Jesus tells the Pharisees, who want him to silence his disciples, that if his disciples are muted, the rocks will still cry out (Luke 19:39-40). The silent suffering and repressed frustration in many of our marriages has left the rocks crying out a message of hope through grace and redemption. As we examine each rock in detail, try to put yourself in the sandals of the biblical heroes. Imagine the circumstances and challenges in which each finds himself. Just as important, consider how the faith lesson presented to each of our heroes applies to your own marriage.

The *Marriage ROCKS* acronym symbolizes the five steps God offers to transform your marriage. The five letters, *R-O-C-K-S*, represent the grace that will make you a conqueror; winner takes all. These letters stand for *Redemption (R)*, *Offering (O)*, *Covenant (C)*, *Knowledge (K)*, and *Sacred Space (S)*. Each of these letters will point the way to authentic marriage by offering theological meaning as the foundation for building meaningful relationships. I am confident that as you read through these chapters, engage in the discussion questions at the end of each chapter, and remain prayerful for insight as a couple or as part of a small group, that God will show you the miracle of authentic marriage.

Top Ten Tips on How Best to Benefit from Marriage ROCKS

Marriage ROCKS is a method or a lens, if you will—a way of looking deeply at one's identity and purpose from three (personal, marital, and communal) God-focused angles. The ultimate goal is to discover exactly why God had marriage in the plans for your life. There is no quick, easy answer to this search. Any book that promises this to you is a farce. The real discovery is in what you bring to the book. This book relies upon biblically based stories of people just like you to serve as a guide for reflection and interaction. These moments of contemplation—whether they happen in your personal time of reading, in a chapter exercise with your spouse, or in group exercises—hold the true answers for your marriage. I do, however, want to be fair. Some of these questions and exercises may be too much for you to handle, based on the state of your marriage or maybe on your own personality. If this describes you, I encourage you just to relax and do your best. God will reward your effort.

Your *Marriage ROCKS* journey will be a more rewarding experience for you as you consistently apply the following ten tips as you progress through this book:

1. Ask trusted family and friends to join you in praying that God will do a supernatural work in your marriage through this *Marriage ROCKS* program.
2. Make a joint covenant with your spouse that you will make your best effort to complete the *Marriage ROCKS* journey.
3. In addition to reading the biblical vignettes upon which the five *Marriage ROCKS* are built, read the entire Bible chapter for a broader perspective of each character.
4. Each chapter contains a Reflection Point. Keep a journal with your responses to each one. Writing in this manner helps to solidify the concepts in your mind.

5. Each chapter presents the story of a couple that is dealing with some aspect of the concepts presented in that chapter. These couples are fictional. However, their stories present realistic composites of relevant issues that African American marriages face. Read each couple's story, and consider the similarities with your own story.

6. Take the time to thoughtfully complete each of the chapter's I ROCK exercises in your personal journal.

7. Set aside time (as uninterrupted as possible) with your spouse to thoughtfully complete each chapter's We ROCK activities.

8. Start or join a *Marriage ROCKS* small group (three to six couples) for the twelve-step journey. Use the *Marriage ROCKS* Leader's Guide to navigate the group discussion and exercises for each chapter.

9. Complete all twelve steps in order as they appear in this book (but feel free to spend as much time on each step as necessary to confidently grasp the concepts taught).

10. Stay encouraged throughout the journey, even when you feel frustrated with yourself, your spouse, your group, or with God.

I ROCK Exercises

Scripture Memorization: 2 Chronicles 20:15, NRSV

He said: "Listen, all Judah and inhabitants of Jerusalem, and King Jehoshaphat: Thus says the LORD to you: 'Do not fear or be dismayed at this great multitude; for the battle is not yours but God's.'"

Contemplation

Respond to the following points of contemplation in your personal journal:

1. Consider your marriage right now. Is it moving toward God or away from God? In your journal write your response and give as many reasons as possible explaining why this is your belief. After considering your responses, write how you feel about your answers.

2. What do you desire to be the legacy of your marriage?

3. What will it take from you personally to accomplish your desired legacy?

Integration

4. Using only a few paragraphs, write a letter to your spouse describing how you think God sees your marriage. Be sure to include the strengths and areas for improvement. NOTE: Avoid any self-blame or blaming of your spouse.
5. In the same letter to your spouse, communicate in your own words your commitment to actively participate in the *Marriage ROCKS* twelve-step program, and what you hope to gain from the process.

We ROCK Exercises

Contemplation

1. Exchange personal letters that you wrote for each other as described in the I ROCK section. Discuss your respective views on your marriage.
2. In preparation for Group ROCK (if you are journeying through *Marriage ROCKS* with a small group), read Luke 15 together. In each Luke 15 parable, the community is called together to rejoice and celebrate when that which was lost is discovered. How might Jesus' message promote involving your community as you celebrate milestones in your marriage?

Integration

3. Take a trip alone or together to the greeting card shop of your choice and pick out a single card for your spouse that states or implies what you most loved about him or her when you first got married—or create a card to convey the same idea. Schedule at least thirty minutes of uninterrupted time alone to exchange and discuss cards.
   - Do NOT share the card with your spouse until you are back home.
   - Do NOT choose a sex-related card.

CHAPTER 2

Choosing Suitability over Compatibility

You were made by God and for God—and until you
understand that, life will never make sense.
—Rick Warren

As a teen and young adult, I often thought about what my wife was going to be like. Given the marital struggles that I saw my own parents fight through, I thought the key was finding someone who was compatible with me. I then proceeded to make a list of the attributes I thought would make Mrs. Right. I figured I am a good Christian of above-average intelligence with good earning potential. So, I wanted a wife with these same attributes. I love playing sports, having a good time with friends, and being involved with church activities. So, I wanted a wife who enjoyed the same activities. Once you add on my desire for someone who was good in the bedroom and in the kitchen (that is, sex in the bedroom and food in the kitchen), I was convinced that this person would be my perfect match. In other words, my sense of the right person for me was to find someone pretty much just like me. That was my definition of compatibility.

Matchmaking services like eHarmony have their own "scientific" algorithm for calculating compatibility. While I am positive that this approach surpasses my old formula for accuracy, I still wonder if calculated compatibility points are a good barometer for capturing the type of person whom God has for you. This is not a knock on dating services at all. I personally believe they serve an important role in our culture. But, I think we should always filter this "scientific" match through God's lens. How do we do that as African American people? We first must understand the nature of God's perspective as contrasted with our own.

A Matter of Perspective

It all starts with perspective. Each of us has a perspective, a way of seeing and explaining our lives. This vantage point helps us to understand ourselves and our spheres of influence in relationships, work, worship, and play. While we tend to believe that our perspectives are commonsense and intuitive, reality is more complicated. The widely differing perspectives that distinct individuals bring to the simplest of issues are each a mix of personal knowledge, beliefs, and experiences. Our perspectives are complex and necessarily biased, and this is often confusing to others.

Let's take a common example in the African American dating scene. African American women often complain about the unavailability of eligible African American men. From their perspective, the prevalence of incarceration, joblessness, and homosexuality among the African American male population limits their ability to find husbands. When you talk to single African American men, however, they lament about African American women who are too materially focused, egotistical, and unwilling to submit to the man as the head of the house. Don't get me wrong. Both perspectives have fallacies and merits. My point is simply that each gender has a simple and convenient explanation for something that is multifaceted and complex.

When it comes to marriage, two (and often more) personal perspectives must coexist in harmony. While this harmonious existence seems easiest to attain during the honeymoon period, the daily routines that follow often put your perspective at odds with that of your spouse. How many arguments have you had recently with your spouse over who is "right"? What is confusing and irritating between friends or work colleagues can be infuriating in our partners. This marital strife exists because one or both partners desperately desire to prove that their perspective is indeed the only correct one. Is it possible that multiple perspectives of a situation are all correct (or all incorrect)? Of course it is. Why, then, do we need to validate the truth of our perspective at the expense of our spouse's perspective? The answer often revolves around the dynamics of control. Of course, we want to be in control of the events around us. This is quite natural. But, here is the problem: God calls us to relinquish control. We are expected to submit our own wills to the purposes of God. In other words, our personal perspectives must be replaced by a God-centered perspective. Who is better able to control your marriage, you or God? The question is intended to be rhetorical, but in reality, how often does God's perspective take a back seat to your own? Genesis 2 provides a third lens through which we can understand God's view for a marriage of two potentially clashing perspectives. God's perspective, I suggest, centers on two interrelated precepts: partnership and covenant. Before we can embark on this journey of marital discovery, we must grasp these foundational concepts.

Partnership

How confident do you feel that your marriage is on track to accomplish all that God has planned for it? Answering this question requires you to see your marriage the way God sees it. This requires a trip back through Scripture to the book of Genesis. Here, God outlines his perspective through his account of the creation of humanity and the first husband-wife team. The Lord places the first human, Adam, in a marvelous garden of perfection and beauty designed for eternal communion with his Creator. What could be more ideal? Yet, even within this utopian existence, God makes the profound yet mysterious proclamation in Genesis 2:18, "It is not good that the man should be alone." This raises two additional questions:

- Why did God say Adam was alone?
- Why was it not good for Adam to be alone?

Adam was in direct fellowship with God and surrounded by the creatures of the Earth, which God had tasked him to name

(Genesis 2:19). Yet, God characterizes Adam as being alone. This is an important truth for our lives and marriages: God is saying that being in the presence of God is not enough. We can still feel lonely. If, therefore, it is possible to feel lonely even in God's presence, how much more can we feel isolated in our marriages?

It is one of the sad surprises of marriage that it is possible to be married and yet feel alone and lonely, despite what appear to be constant activities at home, school, and church. We are often unaware of the isolation that many married persons experience on a daily basis. The Bible does not say that Adam felt alone. Unlike those of us who live after the Fall, Adam had no emotional, psychological, or physical problems. Adam was not anxious about relationship problems or fretting with bouts of anger over perceived injustice. There is no biblical account of Adam complaining or feeling sorrowful about being alone. So, why does God view Adam's situation as less than good?

Genesis 2:20 provides some insights. It seems reasonable that, when faced with the daily responsibility of naming every species on earth, Adam may have questioned why a male and female type existed for each of God's creatures except him. Did Adam sense that something was missing?

God's standard for creation, according to Genesis, is perfection. God declares the entirety of creation to be "very good" (Genesis 1:31). There were no flaws, mistakes, or omissions. Therefore, upon observing that Adam's aloneness is not good, God must act consistently with his own nature. So God immediately states, "I will make a helper suitable for him" (Genesis 2:18, NIV).

The Hebrew-Greek Key Study Bible provides the insight that the term *helper* is translated from the Hebrew root *neged*, meaning *counterpart*, which is apparently the necessary ingredient in achieving perfection. Interestingly, God establishes that being the counterpart assumes *suitability*, a term that is very familiar to our culture. It is important to take note of the word *suitable*. Our self-centered perspectives often cause us to err in determining what is suitable. For us, suitability focuses on temporal aspects such as physical attraction, career aspirations, and education level.

My own "desires for a wife" checklist is a prime example of this self-centeredness. Don't get me wrong. There is nothing inherently wrong with having preferences. We all have them. But this is not God's focus. God's perspective of suitability is about maturing us toward his image. In other words, God places our spouses in our lives to make us suitable for his service. It is upon this premise that I suggest that we replace our reliance on what I will call compatibility with a perspective based on suitability. Compatibility is temporary, while suitability is eternal. Compatibility is selfish, while suitability is selfless. Since the days of creation, God's lens of authentic partnership has been about suitability.

> **Compatibility is temporary, while suitability is eternal. Compatibility is selfish, while suitability is selfless. Since the days of creation, God's lens of authentic partnership has been about suitability.**

Eve was created in the image of God, as was Adam. By juxtaposing the part (Adam) with the counterpart (Eve), God models his perfect plan as entailing *partnership*. God intends for you and your spouse to be suitable partners. Are you ready to abandon your own expectations for a compatible partner, in order to adopt God's intent for your marriage?

Only the Lord can transform your perspective of marriage from temporal self-centeredness to eternal partnership. Only through God's perspective can you echo about your own spouse Adam's words of divine partnership, "This at last is bone of my bones and flesh of my flesh" (Genesis 2:23, NRSV). Therefore, a transforming view of partnership requires being open to learning why God finds you and your spouse suitable. This may be challenging when you feel, at times, that there is no one on earth less suitable for you than the person you actually married!

Covenant

In our Christian lexicon, the term *partnership* is often confused with another word, *covenant*. We tend to think of *partnership* and *covenant* as interchangeable terms, but this interpretation is limiting. While both *partnership* and *covenant* refer to a level of spousal commitment, they differ in meaningful ways. As noted above, *partnership* concerns God's provision of a counterpart who is suitable to help shape you into the image of God. The spousal commitment entailed in partnership is crucial.

Covenant, a more complex concept, is the process that differentiates Christian marriage from secular contract. Godly marriages commit to a journey outlined in Genesis 2:24 (NRSV): "Therefore a man leaves his father and his mother and clings to his wife, and they become one flesh." God describes this first marital partnership as a three-step process of leaving, cleaving, and becoming one. Leaving and cleaving are necessary prerequisites for becoming one. The process of becoming forms the basis for what we understand as covenant. So, on our way to defining covenant, let's examine the interim steps of leaving and cleaving.

Leaving

Christians have traditionally understood *leaving* as the physical departure from one's family of origin to begin a new life with one's spouse. In the time and culture in which Genesis 2:24 was penned, families tended to live in close proximity to one another. In most instances, newly married couples simply lived in the same home as the husband's family or, at most, in the next tent. So, while this interpretation of Scripture certainly holds a simplistic appeal, God's message of leaving must be broader than the physical separation from one's parents.

What other forms might leaving take? It may be that Scripture requires a kind of psychological departure from one's parents. This interpretation is consistent with contemporary studies of the couple process. God's instruction to leave may be understood as a command to psychologically release that which is familiar, taking a step of faith outside one's comfort zone. The end of the familiar is often the point at which our reliance upon the Lord is most necessary, and reliance on the Lord is especially necessary for couples that are struggling.

HOW COMFORTABLE are you when you enter unfamiliar territory? When faced with that which is unfamiliar, what is your typical reaction? One's reaction tends to be very driven by his or her personality. Some people see this experience as invigorating while others shrink back with fear. Write down some major instances in your life with your spouse when you were faced with the unfamiliar. What feelings did you have? How, if at all, did your faith in the Lord impact your decision?

There is an adage that says, "If you keep doing what you've done, you'll keep getting what you've gotten." If your marriage is like most, many of its problems result from an unwillingness to leave certain patterns of thinking and behaving behind. We wonder why God has not delivered us from certain challenges in our marriage. God may be waiting for us to make the decision to leave—not the marriage, but the emotional processes of our families of origin.

I grew up in a home with two parents who loved me. But, my parents differed widely in their ways of showing love. My father, Harold Sr., showed love to me by playing with me (wrestling, basketball, and football), giving me money, and providing food and shelter. My mother, Dorothy, displayed her love for me by pushing me (usually through criticism!) to be the best at almost anything that I did (especially in school). I had no difficulty leaving the home of my parents as a college-bound eighteen-year-old. In fact, for years, I had looked forward to the day I would leave.

But, it would be many more years before I fully understood what I did not leave behind. I subconsciously took with me the attitudes and behaviors that had helped me survive as the eldest and sole male (at that time) sibling in the Arnold household. Only later could I see the troublesome contributions of sarcasm, biting criticism, and caustic humor to my personality.

I married my wife, Dalia, with these personality quirks firmly in tow. While these destructive characteristics may have been functional in my youth, they held the power to destroy my marriage. Dalia continues to remind me of words and tones that I use that make her feel belittled. While we have discussed the issues enough for her to understand that I do not intend to make her feel devalued, she struggles with my behavior nonetheless, because it causes her pain.

I could adopt (and have at times adopted) the stance that my wife needs to just get over feeling hurt, because after all these years of marriage, she should know that I do not intend to harm her. But, how does this attitude align with God's instructions to leave behind the familiar? Becoming one with Dalia requires that I honestly recognize the baggage in my life that I did not leave behind. Desiring full partnership with Dalia forces me to allow my personality to be shaped by my relationship with her. I submit to this very difficult process because I recognize that God identified her as suitable for me. Similarly, all of us show our commitment to our marriages by leaving behind any aspect of ourselves that hinders our relationship with God and with each other. What is God asking you to leave in order to become one with your spouse? I have found that God's call to leave that which is familiar is often, though certainly not always, communicated to us through our spouses. Are you humble enough to listen to what your spouse is saying?

God asks some of us through our partners to leave behind selfish attitudes and desires. Others must desert bad habits that corrode the marital union, because they cause constant pain and irritation. What are the challenges in your marriage that you are struggling to leave? Familiar patterns of thinking and behaving enabled us to function in the complex, ever-changing, and even frightening family environments we lived in as children. Yet, the familiar cements patterns in us that make it difficult to hear God's call to move or our spouse's cry for help. Therefore, for most of us, the first step in the covenant process—leaving the familiar—is a risky proposition. The Lord comforts us by pronouncing a second step to restore our sense of stability. Any time the Lord asks us to leave something, he always gives us replacement instructions. God tells us how to fill the vacuum created by what we have lost or abandoned. This is the next message of Genesis 2:24: Where do I turn after I have left that which is familiar?

Cleaving

God's second step instructs us to cleave to each other. God's guidance for spouses to cleave to each other speaks to the psychological imperative of intimacy in the marriage rather than solely to the concept of creating a separate home.

The cleaving of Genesis 2:24 is not just a superficial connection between spouses. God challenges us to embrace the transformation and shaping that he desires to do in us by giving us our partner. In the early days of our marriages, we are likely to enjoy the process of learning to conform to our spouse's needs and wants. However, our will to cleave deteriorates, rendering us inept in our efforts to join with our partner. It is at this point in our married lives that we begin to drift apart.

Many husbands and wives have become so disillusioned with marriage that they find it difficult to trust God will bring about something better, thus risking disappointment in both God and marriage. Other marriages have so many accumulated emotional injuries that the spouses reject the notion of cleaving altogether, preferring a safer, parallel relationship where each pursues fulfillment independently. A primary thrust of this book is to help in your discovery of God's hand of restoration in your life. This discovery has both vertical (cleaving to God) and horizontal (cleaving to your spouse) dimensions.

Becoming One

Unlike partnership, which begins on the day of matrimony, covenant is a lifetime process to which you have vowed a commitment. The Genesis 2:24 equation is simple: leaving + cleaving = becoming one. However, the process of living the equation challenges us to the core. No couple has ever become one solely by reciting vows. You may only be fully realizing this now, but your verbal commitment at your wedding wasn't simply signing a contract. It cemented your willingness to undertake whatever is necessary to leave well, cleave well, and become one. Your wedding was the commencement of a journey.

Becoming one is a process. Therefore, I ask that you take a step back and think about whether your marriage is succeeding in terms of leaving, cleaving, and becoming one. What unhealthy habits have you been able to leave behind? In what ways, even small ways, do you and your spouse cleave to each other? It is important to take encouragement from even the most incremental steps of progress.

How do we know when we have achieved covenant-centered oneness? Such unity may be best described in the concluding verse of the second chapter of Genesis, "And the man and his wife were both naked, and were not ashamed" (Genesis 2:25, NRSV). This is powerful imagery! We can guess here, of course, that nakedness is not merely the absence of clothing. Psychologically, it is the absence of secrets, hidden agendas, and defenses. God's picture of the perfect marital relationship is characterized by trust and mutual vulnerability—without shame. Nakedness is transparency. God's idea of marital perfection lies in this nakedness.

I ROCK Exercises

Scripture Memorization: Genesis 2:20 (NIV)

So the man gave names to all the livestock, the birds of the air and all the beasts of the field. But for Adam no suitable helper was found.

Contemplation

Respond to the following points of contemplation in your personal journal:

1. How has your understanding of partnership in marriage changed after reading this chapter?
2. Based on Genesis 2:24, we discussed how covenant entails a three-step process of leaving, cleaving, and becoming one.
   a. What patterns of thinking does God want you to leave behind?
   b. How might your efforts to cleave to God and your desire to cleave to your spouse be related?

c. Secrets, hidden agendas, and defenses can all impede your ability to become one with your spouse. How, if at all, have these challenges eroded trust in your marriage?

Integration

3. Clinicians often examine the family history of their clients to observe interaction patterns and boundaries in a person's past. This exercise is designed to examine a profile of your own family history. You and your spouse will have separate family profiles. The goal is to document the relationships of each of your families going back two generations (to your respective grandparents). This profile will be used at various points throughout this book for further illustrations.

   • **Step 1:** Each of you takes two sheets of lined paper. At the top of one sheet write "Mother" and on the other write "Father."

   • **Step 2:** At the top of the sheet labeled "Mother" write the names of your mother's parents. At the top of the sheet labeled "Father" write the names of your father's parents.

   • **Step 3:** On each page under the names of your grandparents write the names of all of their children—include biological, adopted, foster, and stepchildren if you consider them part of your family (write only one name per row and leave two blank rows after each name). These names will include your own parents as well as your aunts and uncles.

   • **Step 4:** Beside each of the names of your aunts and uncles, write the name(s) of any current or previous spouses, if applicable—include official and common law arrangements.

   • **Step 5:** In the first blank row beneath each of the parties specified in the previous step, write the names of their children (include your name as well as your siblings and cousins).

   • **Step 6:** Underneath each of these names, write the name(s) of any current or previous spouses, if applicable.

   • **Step 7:** Before continuing this exercise, make several copies of both sheets of your family history profile because you will need clean versions at several points in this book.

   • **Step 8:** Label your copies "My Family Marriage History."

- **Step 9:** On each of your sheets, place a star by all the couples who separated, divorced, or never married.
- **Step 10:** Place a square around each couple whom you perceive to be in a healthy marriage.
- **Step 11:** Summarize what your family history profile says about marriage in your family.
  a. What, if any, clues do these family history profiles suggest about your own marriage?
  b. Write a letter to your spouse communicating what you need to leave behind in order to benefit your marriage. Write how you think these issues presently affect your marriage. How might your marriage be different when you leave these concerns behind?

We ROCK Exercises

Contemplation

1. Discuss with your spouse the ways in which your perspectives of marriage are similar. Also, discuss ways in which your perspectives differ. This may include comparing and contrasting experiences of marriages that you observed while growing up.
2. This chapter describes Adam and Eve as part and counterpart respectively, suggesting their suitability for each other. Discuss the aspects of your marriage that you believe God finds suitable. What aspects do you believe God does not find suitable?

Integration

3. Marriage Collage: As a couple, create a collage that shows how you and your spouse are suitable for each other. In other words, your collage should show the ways in which you each shape the other into the person God desires. HINT: Use photos, magazine clippings, and anything else to develop your masterpiece. Keep in mind that this exercise does not have to be deeply spiritual. It should capture your essence as a human couple.

CHAPTER 3

Relinquishing Your Imaginary Marriage

We must accept finite disappointment,
but never lose infinite hope.
–DR. MARTIN LUTHER KING JR.

My wife, Dalia, and I met in our senior year as undergraduate students at Howard University. I had always believed that my eventual wife would be an intelligent, career-focused woman who knew how to take care of a home. I wanted a wife who valued family highly but was committed to working hard toward established financial goals. Like the Enjoli perfume commercial of the 1970s quipped, I wanted a woman who could bring home the bacon, fry it up in a pan, and never, ever let her husband forget he's a man. Remember my compatibility checklist that I told you about? I wasn't kidding. When I married Dalia, I was certain that she was the embodiment of the perfume commercial. I was convinced that I had struck gold.

Now, before you ladies reprimand me for my chauvinistic imagination, we need to look at the assumptions Dalia brought into the marriage as well. Dalia describes the knight in shining armor whom she thought she was marrying. Fueled by her love of Harlequin romances, Cinderella-like fairy tales, and Hollywood happy endings, Dalia expected her husband to be her protector and rescuer. She imagined a marriage in which her husband prioritized her mental, physical, and emotional well being over his own needs. This means Dalia and I said "I do" with expectations about what the lifetime ahead as a married couple would be. We have had a blessed marriage. But, Dalia failed to live up to the promise of the Enjoli woman, even as I proved unworthy of knighthood, much less shining armor. In many ways, we have worked over the years to deal with the disappointment that ensued as our imagined marriages fell far short of the real one. While the commitment to each other and to God has never wavered, we have both grieved in our own individual ways the loss of long-held expectations.

> **Disappointment is inevitable in life and certainly in marriage. Every spouse struggles with the gap between what he or she expected married life to encompass and what he or she perceives as its reality.**

Disappointment is inevitable in life and certainly in marriage. Every spouse struggles with the gap between what he or she expected married life to encompass and what he or she perceives as its reality. Beliefs—many of them unconscious—that you brought into your marriage formed a powerful imaginary marriage for you. As childish as it may sound, this imaginary marriage causes significant problems for your real marriage.

THINK BACK to the years before you married. If you have been married more than once, take your mind back to before your first marriage. What did you imagine your spouse and your marriage would be like? Write down the ways your current marriage is similar to and different from what you imagined it would be back then. After completing this exercise, search your emotions to discern how you feel about this.

Husbands, if you came into marriage imagining that your wife would share your love of watching professional football, golfing, or jogging—even though she showed no interest in these activities prior to marriage—how disappointed were you when you found out that she passionately hates athletics? Or, wives, imagine your disappointment when your husband dismisses your hopes for joint dance classes, attending church together, or even wanting to have children. The moment when realities bump up against expectations can be jarring, even frightening. Why did I expect Dalia to be the Enjoli woman, and why did she expect me to be a shining knight? It is far too simple to suggest that television commercials and romance novels are responsible. Rather, I suggest three dynamics that foster our imaginary marriages, making authentic, God-centered marriage more difficult: the irony of mate selection, unmet needs, and communication failures.

These dynamics wreak emotional havoc in marriage as they sow seeds of doubt about whether your spouse is (and will continue to be) really there for you in every sense. Left unchecked, they spiral into disrespect, distrust, unhealthy boundaries, and destructive habits that foster conditional (rather than unconditional) commitment. Destroying these enemies of your marriage begins with gaining a better understanding of their natures. We must recognize that often these seeds of discord are planted well before your marriage even begins.

The Irony of Mate Selection

The physiological wiring of the human body is amazing and mysterious. Increasingly, technology enables us to understand the functioning of our basic life ingredient, DNA, and to meditate upon its implications. Yet, scientists can only guess the elements of human attraction. Excellent theories fail to account for the compulsivity with which we search for "a mate with a very particular set of positive and negative personality traits," according to theorist Harville Hendrix.[1] Spouses commonly state that they were attracted to each other because they are alike, but evidence suggests otherwise. Attraction appears to be a function of complementarity rather than similarity. In other words, your attraction is most typically a function of the extent to which you experience your spouse as being something that you are not. This explains why the extroverted husband is attracted to the woman who is so efficient behind the scenes. Or, why the woman with low self-esteem is attracted to the guy who exudes such confidence. These different personality types may be superficially alike, because the individuals may enjoy the same hobbies, share the same field of work, or appreciate the same worship style. Unconsciously, the attraction may be because they imagine and romanticize the "fit" that comes from two complementary forces.

Sandra and Kian were successful young African American professionals who enjoyed talking about and pursuing their respective career ambitions before marriage. They believed their skills and drive would serve them well as they focused on their new, shared goal of providing a stable home for their hoped-for children. Once their three children were born in quick succession, however, all the couple could see were their differences. Kian, who before marriage seemed stable and orderly to Sandra, now seemed like a lunatic control freak who couldn't tolerate a toy left on the floor or an unruly child at bedtime. Sandra, whom Kian had seen as laid-back and relaxed before marriage, became (in his view) a slacker who was content to leave dishes in the sink for days and didn't even always remember to take a shower. Further, each was convinced that his or her own preferred way of negotiating family life was the one and only acceptable way!

Earlier, we talked about God's design for partnership as characterized by the part and the counterpart. God designed us to search for complementarity. Herein lies both the challenge and opportunity of marriage. While couples typically romanticize their differences during courtship, these differences can take on a more destructive tone as the days and years pass. The "behind the scenes" woman who was so attractive to that extroverted gentleman during courtship now becomes frustrating in her chronic disinterest in parties. Or, the wife who struggles with self-esteem is devastated that her super-confident husband will never understand, much less empathize with, her constant struggle to feel valued. These are just two small examples of the irony of mate selection. The very qualities that most attracted us to our spouses are typically the qualities that ultimately cause the most frustration. Is the solution simply to avoid choosing someone who appears to complement you? The frustration that you feel because your spouse does not see, experience, or value things the way you do is important. This frustration represents growth potential because it pushes you to consider alternative ideas that may enrich your own. The reality is that most people struggle to push the limits of their potential because of the discomfort we feel when facing the unfamiliar. When your spouse introduces a different way of looking at circumstances in a supportive manner, each of you is blessed in the exchange. In this way, what began as frustration ultimately fuels purpose. As you share purpose, you discover passion—not only in your relationship with your spouse but also in your pursuit of God.

Unmet Needs

In addition to our often-subconscious search for complementarity, we also seek companions who satisfy primal needs for safety—especially emotional safety. To some extent, most of us have experienced episodes of abuse, neglect, and fears in our families or early life experiences. These negative experiences create a powerful subconscious lens that drives our behavior, attitudes, and sense of confidence. Regardless of the source of those early wounds, we often enter marriage with an unconscious expectation that our spouse is going to be a salve for those emotional hurts. We expect our spouses to offer uninterrupted, unconditional love, which will protect and heal our emotional injuries. We expect our spouses to validate our intrinsic self-worth, regardless of how worthless we feel. In essence, we long for the acceptance from our spouses that we have never before experienced. Although often unspoken, most couples desire marriages in which they feel emotionally nurtured. How emotionally safe do you feel in your marriage?

The challenge is that this need often is not verbalized or even recognized, because so many of these emotional needs originate from our subconscious selves. When we think about our marriages, our thinking naturally tends to gravitate toward the literal, conscious experiences. You may think of quality, excellent or poor; satisfaction, rewarding or disappointing; or goals that you and your spouse have set, such as purchasing a new home in ten years. Unconscious forces, however, are largely responsible for the expectations we have for marriage, for our spouse, and in fact for everyone in whom we expect to trust. Of course, the fact that many of these fears and internalized conflicts remain outside our awareness makes it difficult to articulate them, much less to assess their impact. Therefore, it is seldom an issue of simply asking one's spouse to do things differently and everything will be fine, or Sandra and Kian would have been able to resolve their differences over family life. Our unconscious lenses guarantee an emotionally needy self-centeredness. Our desperation only increases when we realize our spouse is also needy and self-centered and, therefore, not nearly as available to address our needs.

Transforming your marriage from one tossed by unconscious emotions to a purposeful one requires that you understand the emotional needs and language of yourself and your partner. In short, we need to make our unconscious marriages conscious. You must continually check your emotional thermostat, particularly when you find yourself getting "heated" with your spouse's behavior. If you frequently feel negative emotions around certain topics or feel distant from your spouse around certain issues, there may be subconscious needs that are triggering these emotions.

Communication Expectations

Even folks who have never seen the classic 1967 film *Cool Hand Luke* nevertheless know and even quote its most memorable line. Cornered by prison guards late in the movie, a young Paul Newman, as Luke Jackson, flings a final insult to a corrupt establishment, yelling, "What we've got here is failure to communicate."

The words are barely out of his mouth before he is shot. It is a great line in a great movie.

This line applies across the board to marriages. Almost every African American couple whom I have ever counseled offers some version of Luke Jackson's quote as indicative of the problems in their marriage. We are frustrated because we cannot understand what our spouses are saying. We are hurt and discouraged because we feel unheard. Of course, when you said, "I do," your imaginary marriage promised you that this was the person in whom you would confide your deepest needs and thoughts, and your partner would be an empty container that existed for no other purpose than to meet those needs. But now you struggle to share even basic conversation. Do minor issues fuel major arguments? How many disagreements repeat without resolution? How often do you have that "here we go again" feeling?

Subtle gender differences impact this cycle, too. Stereotypically, husbands feel that their wives talk endlessly but fruitlessly, failing to reach any conclusion on the issues they complain about. A husband may believe endless talk about an issue is an invitation to fix, so he offers that fix in a sincere attempt to help his hurting wife (and if he is completely honest, to get her to stop talking about the problem). But that wife is likely to experience her husband's problem-solving as disrespectful to her feelings. Conversely, a husband facing a challenge may consider it a waste of time to talk about the issue for the sole purpose of receiving emotional support, which is what his wife is inclined to offer. What he probably wants is to have the issue resolved. He thus experiences his wife as unsupportive, when her desire to listen is exactly what she would consider supportive in the reverse situation.

See? What we have here is a failure to communicate. Improving your marriage requires a renewed commitment to improving verbal communication. Some of the foundational research, such as the classic work by Deborah Tannen on gender differences in verbal communication can be boiled downed to four key areas with which most of us are familiar: the content, volume, objective, and decision-making value of that communication.[2] Naturally, while differences in these areas represent many marriages, there are just as many exceptions. You will need to assess the degree to which each captures the communication patterns for your marriage and the degree to which the differences manifest along gender lines. Keep in mind that both partners may use communication differently and toward different ends in home, work, or other settings. In attending to subtle gender differences, we are emphasizing the tendencies of intimate, personal conversation.

Content: "What Are You Talking About?"

Content is the topic or what the conversation is about. Broadly speaking, husbands tend to communicate facts first; objective evidence, statistics, and proofs are the final arbiter of right and wrong. Like Sergeant Joe Friday from the TV show *Dragnet*, we husbands say, "Just the facts, ma'am." Communication revolves around the *what* factor. We husbands want answers to two questions: What happened? and What do you want me to do about it? For guys, communication is functional; communication without a clear and accepted purpose may be heard as noise—subject to being dismissed or blocked out.

Unlike their fact-based counterparts, wives tend to communicate based on feelings first. The facts are less important than how the situation makes them feel. While their husbands are asking "what" questions, wives tend to use other questions to help them understand the context of what has happened, such as how an event developed, why it was allowed to happen—and who are the affected parties. Tannen describes this communication difference as rapport talk (for women) and report talk (for men). It is important for husbands to understand that when your wife asks you a "what" question, she may be asking you to tell her everything that you know, believe, and feel about the topic at hand. How many times have you thought you had answered your wife's question only to be asked a long series of follow-up questions to which you have no answer? And your wife is upset that you fail to pay attention to these critical details!

The bottom line is that husbands and wives, like any two individuals of either gender, may differ in what they consider to be the important content of their communication. Communicating feelings generally comes more naturally to women than it does to men. Frequently, men are not socialized to deal with feelings. This makes it difficult for them to be aware of feelings, much less to discuss them articulately. This lack of awareness does not mean that men don't have feelings. In fact, strong feelings lie under the surface and can manifest in ways that are counterproductive. These communication disparities can make it difficult for a couple to be transparent.

Volume: "Can You Hear Me Now?"

Spouses will also differ in the volume of words they use in daily life, which is simply the number of words spoken. For both men and women the majority of words spoken take place on the job, so that when they arrive home from work their word tank is empty. Men are less inclined to be disturbed by this, but it can be a source of chronic frustration for wives.

Women, in short, use words to foster and maintain connection. After a hard day at work and picking up the "second shift" at home, women will still take on the responsibility of initiating connection with their husbands, and language will likely be their tool of choice for the task. Husbands, your wife does not intend to torture you with language. Your wife does not believe that words have to be task-focused to be meaningful. Her words, because they are tokens of her love, are meaningful in and of themselves.

For men, it is more likely that words fit the law of supply and demand. The greater the supply of words spoken, the less valuable each word actually becomes. For men, superfluous words are worthless noise, as noted earlier. However, by conserving words, men believe that they are increasing the potency of the ones that are shared. This makes perfect logical sense for the male mind. Women may operate from the opposite paradigm in intimate conversation. Wives' words are an investment, not a commodity. They invest in what they believe in. When you as a husband fail to communicate, this suggests to your wife that you do not value her enough to invest in her. Husbands, if you notice one day that your wife is talking to you less, this is not a time to celebrate that she finally gets it. In fact, this is a sign that your wife no longer believes in you—a telltale indicator of emotional separation. There is a similar danger for wives. If you continue to flood your husband with what he perceives as meaningless jabber, he will increasingly distance himself from your speech to the point of relishing the time when he is *not* around you.

Objective: "How Am I Supposed to Respond to That?"

Even the fundamental goals of communication frequently differ between husbands and wives. Earlier, we discussed how communication for men is often about function or utility. Men tend to have more of a future or end-goal orientation than their wives. Communication, therefore, is typically about reaching the goal. For women, the objective for communication tends to be more about process. Communication is an experience in itself, to relish for its relational value.

Husbands blow it when we, with the best of intentions, attempt to convert our wives' relational communication into purposive communication. For example, when your wife complains to you about a coworker who makes long personal phone calls at work, how quick are you to offer a simple solution to her problem? Too often, a husband misses golden opportunities to show caring to his wife by listening empathically, because he errantly believes that she wants him to offer a solution (solution-talk). Later, perhaps a solution would be welcome. But first, your wife prefers that you listen and empathize. In talking to you, your wife is investing in you. And, by listening (rather than offering solution-talk) you give your wife a pleasing return on her investment.

So, what might a husband do to show his wife he cares about her? First, identify and reflect your wife's feelings. An empathetic response such as, "That must really be upsetting," is likely to make your wife feel that you are listening to what she is saying and identifying with what she is feeling. This statement engages you in your wife's emotional process rather than short-circuiting her feelings. And, if you feel that you have some great ideas that your wife could try, let her know that you have some solutions if she decides to ask for them. For wives looking for more effective communication with your husbands, warn your husband that you are not looking for solutions. Try, "I want to talk about how crazy Kathy is making me, but I just need to talk about it right now, not fix it." This type of statement clearly asks your husband to turn off his solution-talk. However, if you do want solutions, tell him! By clearly communicating the *goal* of conversation, spouses are better able to appreciate the other's perspective.

Decision Making: "Where Do We Go from Here?"

We have examined three common structural differences (content, volume, and objective) in the ways husbands and wives approach communication. Let's look at the last difference—the ways men and women approach decision making. Dalia and I have had our struggles with this. My analytical, long-term approach was in direct conflict with her emotional, short-term perspective. I, like many men, have always held to the view that a decision, particularly a major one, should be made based on the evidence at hand. By examining and debating the evidence, the best decision could be made—or so I thought. Amazingly, my wife does not share my systematic method to decision making, preferring a negotiation or compromise. In fact, Dalia gets frustrated because it seems to her as if I always have to get my way. It took me years to realize that "the best argument wins" approach has far more utility in the courtroom than in marriage. My litigation style made Dalia a defendant in a legal battle. And, her emotion-laden defense often fell on my deaf ears—I saw Dalia's perspective as irrational. Does this sound at all familiar?

Husbands and wives tend to differ in their experiences as to what constitutes effective decision making—best argument wins vs. negotiating a compromise. Undoubtedly, there are times when decisions should be based strictly on evidence, while other decisions should be based on a combination of factors. The communication failure, however, happens when the couple is not capable of negotiation. Healthy marriage is a blending of two perspectives. If one spouse devalues the importance of compromise (thereby devaluing the partner's opinion and feelings), the Lord's intent for marriage is stunted. Healthy marriage requires that we learn and yield to godly techniques for communication that provide a safe space for negotiation.

Like Kian and Sandra, many of us have difficulty adjusting to the inevitable shifts of marriage—shifts that disrupt the marriages we imagined we would have. Too often the marital adjustments following the birth of a child, the demands of a new job, challenges among our extended families, or some other unplanned events drive a wedge between couples as we struggle to regain a sense of control. In reality, however, it is your imaginary marriage that is controlling you, rather than the other way around. Your liberation comes, as you are able to join as a couple in submitting your real worries and fears to God, the Rock of Salvation.

Marriage, in many ways, is like combat warfare. Disunity is the clearest path to defeat. Your job is to allow the Lord to transform your individual imaginary marriages into a shared vision that affirms each other and glorifies God. This is the simple, yet profound, message of this book. Yes, marriage ROCKS!

As you and your spouse begin to share experiences of redemption, offering, covenant, knowledge, and sacred space, you will discover how to honor marriage as a sacrament. It is here that you can fully appreciate the apostle Paul's words to the church at Ephesus (Ephesians 3:17-20) as he helps them "grasp how wide and long and high and deep is the love of Christ." Paul's words highlight how the Lord promises to do immeasurably more than you can ask or imagine, according to the power that is at work within you. Paul's words are intended to help you see that your imaginary marriage seeks to limit that which God intends to expand.

I ROCK Exercises

Scripture Memorization: Ephesians 4:29

Do not let any unwholesome talk come out of your mouths, but only what is helpful for building others up according to their needs, that it may benefit those who listen.

Contemplation

Respond to the following points of contemplation in your personal journal:

1. Think back to before you married. What did you imagine your relationship would look like? What influenced the expectations that became your imaginary marriage?
2. If your actual marriage has not lived up to your imagined one, how have you dealt with the disappointment of not attaining your goal?

Integration

3. Ask someone who knows you well (e.g., parent, sibling) to give you an honest appraisal of your own communication style. Ask them specifically about areas discussed in this chapter. Try to get them to give you examples when possible. Take notes in your journal.

We ROCK Exercises

Contemplation

1. Discuss with each other what you learned from the interviews that you had in the "I ROCK" section. How similar is your spouse's perspective to those outside opinions?

Integration

2. As a couple, go through each of the ten "rooms" listed below. Compare and contrast your feelings about which room characterizes your marriage's communication pattern.

a. Ball Room: I feel like we are dancers moving in synchronous and harmonious steps.
b. Music Room: I feel like we are in harmony despite a few missed notes.
c. Exercise Room: I feel like even if we sweat a little, we will feel better afterward.
d. Living Room: I feel like our talk sounds good on the surface, but real issues are not being discussed.
e. Family Room: I feel like we get bogged down with family issues rather than talking about us.
f. Game Room: I never feel quite sure whether I can trust my spouse or if I'm being played.
g. Laundry Room: I feel like we are stained clothes that never get fully clean.
h. Court Room: I feel like we are lawyers arguing and defending points.
i. Emergency Room: I feel like we are always dealing with one crisis after another.
j. Boiler Room: I feel like we are furnaces about to overheat.

PART TWO

Discovering Redemption:
The Rock of Grace

Jesus lived and died in vain if he did not teach us
to regulate the whole of life by the eternal law of love.
—Mohandas [Mahatma] Gandhi

Redemption

The Marriage ROCKS journey, like all steps towards Christ, must begin with redemption. In our sinful state we are incapable of loving our spouses the way God commands us. We often stumble and flail in our attempts, as our own egos and shortsightedness render us more self than other-focused. Redemption, however, promises hope. Redemption is the hope that through Christ's grace we can learn to identify our own faults and sacrifice ourselves for our spouses in ways that honor the sacrifice that Christ made for us.

David said to the Philistine, "You come against me with sword and spear and javelin, but I come against you in the name of the LORD Almighty, the God of the armies of Israel, whom you have defied. This day the LORD will hand you over to me, and I'll strike you down and cut off your head. Today I will give the carcasses of the Philistine army to the birds of the air and the beasts of the earth, and the whole world will know that there is a God in Israel. All those gathered here will know that it is not by sword or spear that the LORD saves; for the battle is the LORD's, and he will give all of you into our hands."

As the Philistine moved closer to attack him, David ran quickly toward the battle line to meet him. Reaching into his bag and taking out a stone, he slung it and struck the Philistine on the forehead. The stone sank into his forehead, and he fell facedown on the ground.

So David triumphed over the Philistine with a sling and a stone; without a sword in his hand he struck down the Philistine and killed him. (1 Samuel 17:45-50)

CHAPTER 4

Step 1: Confront the Enemies of Your Marriage

To forgive is to set a prisoner free and
discover that the prisoner was you.
–Lewis B. Smedes

Redemption: To Cover from Guilt

The message of redemption is the centerpiece of Scripture. Since the disobedience of the first married couple, humankind has struggled in ways requiring redemption. It should be no surprise, then, that redemption is the starting point in our journey to marital authenticity.

As Christians we use the term *redemption* quite liberally. But, do we really stop to think about what it means? We can fully appreciate the biblical vignette of David and Goliath as we wrestle with the concept of redemption both theologically and practically.

As African Americans in general and as married couples specifically, we have issues that need healing through redemption. Systematic injustices inflicted upon us as a people have left psychological, economic, and relational wounds that remain unhealed. It would be naïve for us to think that these prejudices have not impacted our marriages. Our challenge is to begin, as a community, to make more widespread gains in the battle for healthy marriages. This battle is only won when we earnestly extend God's banner over our marriages.

Let's revisit our vignette of David and Goliath for insights to help us achieve our objective of an authentic marriage. The message of redemption begins with the understanding that God is completely holy and, therefore, cannot permit anything or anyone into his presence that is not also completely holy. Yet, there the unholy giant stood. David was fully aware of the fact that God would not stand for Goliath's defiance, even as David listened to Goliath's taunts. David became incredulous that an uncircumcised Philistine could render the Lord's army helpless.

David's emphasis on circumcision was not merely a clever insult. Circumcision was the special practice of the Lord's people as a testament to their faith and dedication to Yahweh. So, when David asks, "For who is this uncircumcised Philistine that he should defy the armies of the living God?" (1 Samuel 17:26, NRSV), he is making a theological statement that appears to have been lost on the Hebrew army. David's question is rhetorical. He is asking, "How can this unclean and unholy man stand in the face of a holy God?" Because he is uncircumcised, Goliath is not protected by God's redemptive covering. David's logical conclusion, then, is that God will remove Goliath from God's holy presence. It therefore follows, in David's mind, that the only question is *how* God's purposes will be advanced.

In this chapter, we will emphasize the single stone David used to destroy Goliath. In the Old Testament perspective, the one stone is Yahweh. For David, this single stone was the Rock, encompassing divine power, divine presence, and divine knowledge. For we who live in the age of grace, this stone represents the Chief Cornerstone, Jesus Christ. Despite forty days of gripping fear and paralyzing lack of faith among the Hebrew army, God covered their shortcomings with a single stone. That stone we shall call *redemption*: the stone that promises healing for African American marriages. First, a brief recap to highlight the role of Jesus Christ as Redeemer.

In Chapter 2, we examined the impact of sin's introduction to humanity in general and into the marital relationship more specifically. Human depravities render us defective and incapable of having a direct relationship with God or fulfilling God's intent for the husband–wife union. Without intercession, humankind is separated from God for eternity. For this reason, God implemented an intervention—a plan of redemption to cover our guilt. God's redemptive plan resulted in himself coming to earth in the form of a man named Jesus. Jesus was born of a virgin and lived a perfect life in order to take upon himself the sins of the world. In this way, we understand Christ as our Redeemer. Christ ushered redemption into our human consciousness. However, Christ is the Redeemer only for those individuals who forsake their right to live by their own precepts and who seek forgiveness for transgressions. Christ's death continually covers our guilt, so that we can have access to God's throne despite our human failings. Redemption is the most powerful force in the world, because it represents the loving care and grace of the LORD for his children. It is this force that seals the love and grace in your marriage as well.

Part of God's redemption story is the possibility, I believe, that the very conflict that Satan intends to use to destroy us is exactly what God chooses to use to mature our marriages into partnership and covenant.

Redemption in Marriage

No one enters marriage fully mature. Some individuals may have qualities such as temperament, insight, or specific wisdom which can soothe or de-escalate points of marital friction. But, it is inevitable that all marriages will experience conflict. Part of God's redemption story is the possibility, I believe, that the very conflict that Satan intends to use to destroy us is exactly what God chooses to use to mature our marriages into partnership and covenant. This God-centered perspective is sometimes complex to understand because conflict can make it difficult, even impossible, for you to see your spouse the way God does. The story of Rob and Jeanette in the sidebar highlights the importance of redemption in marriage.

Rob and Jeannette met and married before they were twenty. At not-quite-forty years of age, they had six children and two grandchildren, a successful business, and a good life together.

When an incident of gang violence ended with the murder of their son-in-law in their inner-city home (witnessed by their younger children), Jeannette's grief and anger overwhelmed her. When she sought Rob for comfort in her distress, he—a man much more comfortable with the calm, rational wife he had been married to for over twenty years—withdrew. This fueled Jeannette's pain, which made her pursuit of comfort even more desperate, causing further withdrawal by Rob. Rob, like many African American men, refused to participate in couples' counseling. Even though Jeannette begged him to seek counseling with her, Rob claimed the problem was all Jeannette's. This cycle escalated for two years, until Rob began drinking at home and after work, often arriving home long after their teenage kids were in bed, yet denying that there was anything unusual about this behavior. Jeannette eventually asked Rob to leave, because his unpredictability and unavailability were disrupting life, not just for Jeannette but for the entire family.

We are challenged, like David, to respond to the Lord's desire to remove unholiness from God's divine presence. David's passion for the Lord motivated him to take ownership of the issue. Many marriages, however, assume the sulking posture of the Hebrew army—giving up without ever having fought the battle. Jeannette was begging Rob to engage his passion for his marriage and to fight the battle against their family tragedy with her, but his unwillingness ultimately ended this marriage. Are you willing to face the difficult challenges of marriage, so that God may be glorified in their outcomes?

Agape: A Case for Redemption in Marriage

Dalia tells everybody that I love gadgets. She is right. I enjoy researching and, when possible, purchasing the latest audio, video, and ancillary entertainment toys. When I finally make a purchase, I must then decide whether I want the extended warranty offered by the salesperson. I typically buy it for more expensive items, because if anything goes wrong, I want a new gadget with no questions asked. I want the equipment to work the way it was designed to work.

Like a damaged electronic gadget, we humans no longer work as designed. Our defects allow our fears and frustrations to dominate our thinking and influence our behavior. However, Christ the Redeemer offers us the ultimate extended warranty—one for which he has already paid the price. We live in an age of grace in which Christ's death allows our individual and marital errors to be forgiven by the Lord. But, Christ's extended warranty does not end there; it also provides the framework for human forgiveness. Colossians 3:13 instructs us, "Bear with each other and forgive whatever grievances you may have against one another. Forgive as the Lord forgave you." The Lord models forgiveness for us. His expectation is that we extend to each other the same grace he extends to us. Failing to be gracious to your spouse actually inhibits God's ability to be gracious to you. Jesus demonstrates this in the book of Matthew.

Jesus told his disciples the parable of the unmerciful servant (Matthew 18:21-35), in which the king forgave the debt of a servant who owed him a large sum of money. Rather than selling the servant and his family into slavery, the king extended grace based on the servant's plea for forgiveness. Later, this servant came upon another man who owed him a small sum; yet, he refused to extend grace and had the man imprisoned for non-payment. When the king heard this, he immediately ordered the servant tortured until he could pay the formerly forgiven debt. Jesus explains this parable as the manner in which the Heavenly Father will treat each of us if we fail to extend grace to one another.

JESUS' PARABLE of the unmerciful servant provides insight for many African American couples. When your husband fails to contribute his fair share to the marriage or when your wife prioritizes the needs of others over yours, do you offer to him or her the same grace that God shows you? What could you do to better align the grace you give with the grace you receive?

Here is the essential message of Jesus' parable: The extension of the Lord's grace in marriage hinges upon the grace you offer to your partner when he or she sincerely asks for forgiveness. Often, you will feel like your spouse does not deserve this grace, so remember, neither do you deserve the grace that the Lord extends to you. *Grace*, by definition, means unmerited favor. Grace always involves giving something that is not earned or deserved. Grace is sacrifice.

What about those instances when your spouse denies that he or she has done anything offensive or those times when forgiveness is not followed by any change in a behavior? These difficult scenarios are common, particularly in distressed marriages. In these difficult situations, one of the practices of the Amish may provide insight for you.

Forgiveness: The Way of the Amish

The Amish way of life is an enigma to many in American culture. While some of their practices, such as shunning wayward insiders of the community, seem contradictory to the inclusiveness embraced by the African American subculture, there is, paradoxically, a practice of forgiveness that is ingrained in their religious practices. Simply put, when transgressed by an outsider they offer forgiveness regardless of the offender's behavior, recognizing that forgiveness liberates them from the negative effects of harbored hate. It is a form of emotional release that is foreign to the conventional American mindset, primarily because it centers upon their stance with God rather than upon their rights. This approach came into stark focus on October 2, 2006, in Lancaster County, Pennsylvania, when a gunman named Charles Carl Roberts took hostages at an Amish school, eventually killing five schoolgirls before killing himself. This tragedy, which grabbed national headlines for days, is inexplicably heinous; the lives of innocent children were cut short because of the nonsensical actions of one person. These children's families had every right to hate Mr. Roberts. But, before the evening was over, a spokesperson for the families went to the family of Mr. Roberts to offer forgiveness. We all wonder how it is possible to forgive such an atrocity. It centers upon a way of thinking, believing, and immersing ourselves in the power of God's unconditional love—love that redeems that which seems unworthy of redemption. To what degree can you love your spouse this way?

Spousal Redemption

Spousal redemption is helping our respective spouses, by covering their failings, to become the person God has purposed them to be. When you offer a covering to your spouse, you are her primary advocate when others doubt her; you have faith in him when other people do not; you are willing to forgive his contrite heart when others cannot; you have her back against would-be perpetrators; you extend yourself to make amends for his inadvertent (and sometimes deliberate) transgressions. Regardless of how unreasonable or unrealistic these redemptive acts sound, Christ modeled all of these. Christ advocates for us before God, the Father. Christ recognizes the strengths within you when others doubt you. Christ offers forgiveness to you when others cannot.

Let's look more closely at spousal redemption. The apostle Paul captures its spirit in his poetic description of agape love in his first letter to the Corinthians:

> Love is patient, love is kind. It does not envy, it does not boast, it is not proud. It is not rude, it is not self-seeking, it is not easily angered, it keeps no record of wrongs. Love does not delight in evil but rejoices with the truth. It always protects, always trusts, always hopes, always perseveres. Love never fails (1 Corinthians 13:4-8).

The case for redemption in marriage clearly centers on this agape model that the Bible says never fails.

HOW CLOSELY DOES your love for your spouse align with the apostle Paul's admonition in 1 Corinthians 13? Paul asserts that the fruit of this love should yield feelings of security, trust, and hope in your marriage. Write down some things you can do for

your spouse within the next seven days to demonstrate an aspect of the apostle Paul's guidance.

Now that you have a sense of what spousal redemption entails, let us also state what redeeming your spouse is not. We cannot confuse participating in God's redemptive power in our spouse's life with our own power. We can participate in God's redemption, but we cannot cause it. As stated before, only God through Jesus can redeem us. Therefore, spousal redemption never involves condoning something that God deems sinful, such as violence, extramarital affairs, or a denied addiction. Redeeming your spouse never means that you discount your spouse's transgressions or their impact on you and those you love. In fact, a key aspect of redemption is that you hold your spouse accountable for their behavior just as the Lord holds each of us responsible for our own.

Of course, it is not easy modeling agape love, for it necessitates yet another call to sacrifice. Your own struggles and insecurities may leave you feeling ill-prepared for the task. You may instinctively want to chasten rather than show charity, because you have been hurt too often by the offenses. Too often, I have used my wife's weaknesses and missteps to get my own way rather than looking for opportunities to extend redemption to her.

It is possible to forgive a partner and to allow natural consequences of offenses to follow. Consider the couple in which the husband's affairs have resulted in his contracting a venereal disease. It is appropriate in this situation for the wife to request a separation until the disease has been treated and to require proof from a doctor that it has been treated. Then she must decide if she is willing to continue the relationship based on what this disease may require of her. (Some venereal diseases can be treated but never cured; therefore, there is a perpetual requirement to engage in "safe sex" thereafter, which can limit but not guarantee protection from exposure.)

Or, consider the couple in which the wife has been an active alcoholic for years. Finally, when he's no longer able to rationalize the negative impact on the family, her husband meets her at the door with two suitcases and a choice: she goes to rehab or he and the kids are going to his parents' home until she decides to do something about her drinking problem.

Love is patient and kind, but it cannot be confused with enabling deep, systemic, recurrent issues in a partner's life. Sometimes the kindest love is what some would call "tough love." The key is motive. Are you using tough love as an excuse to punish, or do you honestly and humbly see it as the only hope of eventual redemption? We are required by Scripture to forgive, but we are not responsible for the redemption of a partner whose brokenness prevents him or her from receiving the covering of our love.

Real life issues of forgiveness are difficult because trust and confidence have been breached. Even when we work to forgive, our fears of further betrayal may cause us to become more insecure and controlling. When transgressions blemish your marriage, it is only through God that authentic redemption can take place, as the power of the Holy Spirit facilitates the change necessary for healing to ensue. Can you believe that nothing is too hard for God? The promise of God's provision was sufficient for David to attack Goliath, the enemy of God's people, with confidence in victory. Victory is yours as well as you remain confident in God's provision for healing and restoration.

I ROCK Exercises

Scripture Memorization: Colossians 3:13

Bear with each other and forgive whatever grievances you may have against one another. Forgive as the Lord forgave you.

Contemplation

Respond to the following points of contemplation in your personal journal:

1. What areas of your marriage does Satan hold hostage? Where is redemption most needed in your marriage?
2. Forgiveness is the heart of redemption. What are the emotional wounds that your spouse has inflicted upon you? Which ones are most difficult to forgive? How can you use this pain to strengthen your relationship with the LORD and with one another?

3. Forgiveness in marriage is often a two-way street. In what areas might you need to repent to God and your spouse for sinful thoughts and actions?

Integration

4. Reflect upon the emotional wounds that you have experienced in your marriage (or those that you have experienced in general that are impacting your marriage). Write down the three strongest feelings by filling out the following sentence: My emotional wounds make me feel (1) _____, (2) _____, and (3) _____. Now take some time to reflect on the years before you were an adult. Describe the times (circumstances and people involved) when you most strongly felt the same emotions that you wrote. Can you make any connections? HINT: Sometimes these emotions can be hard to identify because our minds "protect" us from them. Do not feel rushed. If the emotions feel overwhelming, you may want to consider visiting with a professional counselor or therapist.

We ROCK Exercises

Contemplation

1. To the extent that you each feel comfortable, discuss the emotional wounds that you have caused each other (or maybe the areas where you each could be more sensitive to the other's emotional needs). Do not defend yourself. Just listen.

Integration

2. Pick one or more of the following three movies, and watch it together: *Marvin's Room, The Fisher King, The Straight Story*. Although these movies are not about marriage, they each tell a story of redemption. How might the movie(s) that you watched speak to issues of forgiveness and redemption in your marriage? NOTE: If you prefer not to watch a movie, choose a book, play, or other work with redemption as the underlying theme.

CHAPTER 5

Step 2: Exchange Guilt for Grace

Who you are is more important than what
you do when it comes to communication.
—LES AND LESLIE PARROTT

What does the redemptive stone mean for your marriage? Everything. Just as hurt people hurt people, redeemed people redeem people. Climbing the redemptive stone in your marriage cannot begin until you become more comfortable with vulnerability and transparency in your marriage. This is often a painstaking process, because of the disappointments and even abuse that we have experienced. But, as you are able to push through the challenges of unmet needs and communication failures, you will discover heightened levels of marital partnership built upon redemption and sanctification. It is this very struggle that shapes you for God's purpose.

**Spousal redemption starts with
your relationship with God, not with
your relationship with your spouse.**

Climbing the redemptive stone in marriage is a process of four movements: repentance to God, repentance to your spouse, forgiveness of your spouse, and, finally, redemption of your spouse. As we examine this process, it is imperative to stay focused on one key point. Spousal redemption starts with your relationship with God, not with your relationship with your spouse. Whether you are the victim or the culprit, it is to God that you must turn with an open heart (and mind). My grandmother used to say, "Make sure you get right with God." Truer words were never spoken when it comes to redemption in marriage.

The First Movement: Repentance to God

All redemption begins with God. Our Christian belief system centers upon the covering that God provides through Jesus. Not only did God cover our sins by his gracious act of sacrifice, but God modeled the means by which we redeem one another. Climbing the redemptive stone in your marriage first requires that you find God's redemption for you. If you struggle with your own liberation, you will find it difficult to liberate your spouse. If your own internalized guilt and shame make you feel unworthy to ask for God's forgiveness for your own transgressions, then you are likely closed to hearing your spouse's request for forgiveness. Further, if you are unable to accept that there is some transcendent purpose for which your marriage is designed, you are likely to settle for the mundane rather than pushing for the miraculous. Your marriage is a human endeavor that is framed by a divine covenant between God and God's people. It isn't just about you. The Christian marriage covenant is about you in relationship with God and your spouse.

Our first step in climbing the redemptive stone in marriage is seeking forgiveness from God for the ways that we have transgressed the covenant each couple forms during the marriage ceremony. As you repent to God, you are not merely speaking words; you are assuming a posture. This posture is one of humility and acknowledging your faults. It recognizes your own frailties and miscues in the marriage. Repenting to God means that you, individually, acknowledge responsibility for many (not all) of the challenges in your marriage. Yet, repentance to God indicates hope—hope that extends beyond your understanding and hope that believes in that which may not be evident. It is the essence of faith—the belief that God has brought you and your spouse together for a lifelong commitment and, as such, Christ is redeeming that commitment when your marriage is turned over to him.

The issues with which you struggle—the incompatibilities, the unmet needs, and the communication disconnects—are all part of the maturation process that will ultimately make you stalwarts of marriage. Repentance to God recognizes that the success you find in marriage is not of your own doing but is through the continued extension of God's grace.

If you are not sure how to repent to God for your marriage, do not be intimidated. Prayer is never just in the words that you speak. Prayer is the state of your heart and your posture before the Lord. Take a few minutes with the Lord to offer this simple prayer of repentance, but do so only as you feel the Spirit of God tugging on your heart for a more personal commitment to your marriage.

Dear Lord,

I acknowledge you as my personal Savior. You are my eternal Father, existing before the world began. I come before you with a humble and contrite heart on behalf of my marriage. My past and present experiences have rendered me incapable of being the husband/wife that you have ordained me to be. My sincere desire is to become everything as a person and partner that you created me to be before the foundation of the world. I ask that you forgive me for all of the unconscious and conscious errors that I have made. I ask that you forgive me for the transgressions that I committed because of my action and my inaction. Illuminate the areas of my life that are in need of healing, and be a balm for me. Help me to better understand the partner to whom you have joined me. Help me to see [spouse's] the way that you see [him/her]. Teach me how to communicate with [spouse's] in such a way that [he/she] feels validated and loved. Finally, renew my mind so that I can accept the shaping that you desire for me. Lord, I commit my marriage as an offering to you. Do with it and with me what you will. In the name of Jesus, I humbly offer this petition. Amen.

Now that you have repented to God, you have a blank slate. God is a God of second, third, fourth, and fifth chances. When you pray with a broken and contrite spirit, he will forgive you, but you must also be willing to forgive yourself. You must walk in healing and liberty. God forgives you. But, if you continue to allow your guilt, shame, anger, and disappointment to wreak havoc in your mind, you will be unable to walk in the abundance of God's forgiveness. Satan will bring your past failures and fears to mind. If you wallow in guilt you will be unable to participate in your partner's redemption. Your liberty demands that you repeat the same words that Jesus said, "Get behind me, Satan! You are a stumbling block to me; for you are setting your mind not on divine things but on human things" (Matthew 16:23, NRSV). As God forgives you, forgive yourself.

The Second Movement: Repentance to Your Spouse

After asking for God's forgiveness, seek the forgiveness of your spouse. It is likely that your marriage, like so many others, feels burdened. You have a choice: Either you can continue to accept the way things are, or you can decide to make things different. While you cannot force your spouse to change, you can will yourself to do so. All positive change begins with a decision to prioritize healthy behaviors over unhealthy ones.

I would like to stress the importance of this act of repentance, even if you believe that your marriage is healthy or if you are unable to discern specific reasons why repentance might be necessary. Often, partners are unaware of unspoken injuries to their husbands and wives—your partner may be struggling, and you may not even know it! Through your act of repentance to your partner, you express authentic love as well as commitment to the health of your marriage.

Repenting to your partner is twofold. First, it is a statement acknowledging your own culpability or responsibility for some of your marital struggles, for words or deeds that deliberately or unintentionally injured. Second, it is an apology for these actions and a request for forgiveness. For many, this step will seem unfair and perhaps even insulting. You might ask, "Why should I repent to a spouse who cheated on me and abused me?" It seems unfair and disproportionate. If this has been your experience, you are right. It is unfair. It is, in fact, the same unfairness that God showed when he asked his blameless son, Jesus, to be tortured and to die for you and me. Jesus' death shows us that the question of redemption does not revolve around the issue of fairness and equity. Instead, the beauty and mystery of Jesus' death was simply about a new covenant. The new covenant, applied to marriage, is that I will do for you even though you don't deserve it. Because of this new covenant, humanity's relationship with God shifted from legalistic rules and rituals to authentic relationship; therefore, our marriages can, too.

Our marriages tend to be a compendium of rules, regulations, and loopholes (many of which are part of our imaginary marriage) more akin to a legal brief than a love relationship. Typically, these "legalistic" marriages have the feel of a courtroom, as defendant and plaintiff argue respective points of view. As any marriage therapist will tell you, this is a pointless, damaging dynamic. The key, again, is repentance. You cannot require your spouse to repent for his or her portion of the marital discord. You can only repent on your own behalf. Your act of repentance cannot be initiated with the expectation that your spouse will reciprocate, for in many instances he or she will not.

WE HAVE BEEN DISCUSSING the importance of redemption in marriage. So far, our attention has focused on the areas in your marriage where you have fallen short. Take a moment to pray for insight into your own attitudes and behaviors that need forgiveness. Keep in mind that God knows your heart and your thoughts, even when you believe your behavior is innocent. Write down those things for which you need forgiveness from God and from your spouse.

This reflection point is intended to highlight an irony: the fact that your act of repentance to your spouse is more appropriately understood as an act of contrition to the Lord. It is an act of obedience to God (which is why it is less important whether your spouse reciprocates or even forgives you). As you repent to your spouse for your own missteps, you are actually speaking a new covenant into existence. Your act prioritizes agape (unconditional) love over your own feelings of disappointment, fear, and anger. Your repentance signifies that obedience to God's plan is your governing priority. Regardless of your spouse's response to your repentance, the humility and grace that you offer are honored by God. The key is authenticity; your repentance must be genuine. Insincere efforts will be dismissed by the Lord, and your spouse will doubt your honesty. You may begin the process by asking the Lord to help you be sincere. The sample letter below can serve as a guideline, but make the words your own.

Dear [husband/wife],

I believe that God placed us together for a purpose that transcends us as individuals. Together with God, we form a threefold bond that cannot be easily broken. I have gone before the Lord to repent for the things that I have said and done that have weakened this marriage. I am beginning to better understand how issues from my past, such as my unrealistic expectations and my difficulty communicating in a way that best conveys my feelings and disappointments, have made me less than an ideal partner. I have asked the Lord to continue to show me issues that hinder our marriage. By faith, I believe that he will honor this request. I also want you to know how sorry I am for the errors that I have made in our marriage. Some of these mistakes were intentional; I wanted to hurt you because I was hurting. Other mistakes were unintentional, as I was not sensitive enough to your needs and concerns. With the Lord's help, I commit from this point forward to do my best to become the spouse that God formed me to be. I would like it if, as a couple, we could commit to a regular time of prayer each week. Would you be willing to pray with me?

Remember that these words are just a guide. Notice that all of your statements are personal—you accept responsibility for the hindrances that you knowingly or unwittingly introduced into the marriage. This in no way assumes that only you are responsible for the current state of your marriage. You can only control you. This places the remainder of the burden in the hands of the Lord to deal with in his time. Note that there is no blame assigned to your spouse, as this may put your spouse on the defensive and hinder the movement of the Holy Spirit in this moment. There is no "but" clause at the end of a sincere request for repentance.

The Third Movement: Forgiving Your Spouse

Now that you have repented to God and to your spouse, you must engage in what is typically the most difficult step: forgiving your partner. Depending on the emotional wounds you have suffered at his or her hands, the contriteness and sincerity of your spouse's apology (if offered), and your own sense of self-worth, you may struggle with this step. You may even feel as if you have already forgiven your spouse many times, only to be hurt again by his or her actions. If you are wondering how many times you have to forgive your spouse, Scripture offers us clear insight. The apostle Peter, thinking himself wise, asked in Matthew 18:21 if it was enough to offer forgiveness seven times to someone who had sinned against him. Jesus blew Peter's logic out of the water when he replied that the appropriate number of times to forgive is seventy times seven. Was Jesus suggesting that 490 times is the magic number? No. Jesus replaced a legalistic counting of transgressions with a posture of grace and accommodation. There is no definitive or "right" number of times to forgive your spouse.

Remember, assuming a posture of forgiveness does not imply a carte blanche acceptance of negative behaviors. Nor does this posture of grace suggest that you immediately forgive your spouse's wrongdoing. Sometimes true forgiveness can take years, as emotional wounds heal, circumstances change, and memories fade. Forgiveness cannot be placed on a timetable, no matter how much one wishes it so. Finally, forgiveness does not necessarily mean forgetting.

If forgiving your spouse does not mean acceptance of the behavior or forgetting the actions, what does it mean? First, is your spouse asking to be forgiven? Can you forgive your spouse even if he or she does not ask for forgiveness? Absolutely! Forgiveness is the condition of your heart and mind, as much about easing your emotional burden as your partner's. I pray that your spouse does seek your forgiveness, but in the interim, be empowered to forgive anyway.

When should you abandon the goal of unity? When is enough enough? There is no one-size-fits-all answer. There clearly may be situations in which you or those for whom you are responsible (e.g., children) must be removed from environments that pose physical and psychological harm. There may be situations when your partner fails to acknowledge any responsibility for any problems or solutions in the relationship. There may be other instances in which your partner's attempts at repentance drip with sarcasm and insincerity. In such difficult cases, your efforts to connect with your spouse in this spiritual endeavor will likely be unsuccessful. It is important that you surround yourself with safe people with whom you can pray and intercede for your spouse, for your marriage, and for your discernment. These difficult situations are not cause to lose all hope. Many couples have survived unbelievably strenuous circumstances that ultimately became powerful testimonies of redemption.

If you are in the throes of what feels like a hopeless marriage with an uncaring and insincere spouse, do not abandon these steps of redemption. Honor God by committing yourself to the marriage. But, at the same time, ask God to give you wisdom for how to guard your physical and psychological welfare. Ultimately, your marriage will arrive at the level of purpose and ministry that God desires only when mutual repentance and forgiveness are accomplished. But the issues are not only purpose and ministry. Your marriage will never become all that you have hoped for until sincere efforts at repentance and forgiveness are offered. The next page in this book will provide you with examples for forgiving your spouse in a God-honoring manner. One is to use when your spouse requests forgiveness, and the other is for releasing forgiveness when your spouse does not ask.

Sample Format When Spouse Requests Forgiveness

Dear [husband/wife],

It means a lot to me that you have apologized for your role in the current state of our marriage. Many things that you have done have hurt me deeply. And honestly, I know that it will take me some time to fully forgive them. Other things have emotionally and physically drained me. I also know that there are some things that you said that were absolutely correct. I think we are beginning to realize that we both have contributed to the struggle. Although neither of us has all of the answers, I believe that God has a path and a plan for our marriage that is far beyond what we have experienced thus far. Not only do I accept your sincere apology, but I reiterate my commitment to you and to God. I believe that today is a day that we will remember as a transition point in our relationship. Today is confirmation of the right decision that I made in marrying you.

Sample Format When Spouse Does Not Request Forgiveness

Dear Lord,

My highest priority is to honor you. I have sought your forgiveness for the intentional and unintentional harm that I have caused my marriage. I have asked you to show me ways that I can be a better marriage partner. And, in obedience, I have done my best to apologize to my spouse for these behaviors as well. I recognize that we are both responsible for the difficulties in our marriage. [Spouse's name] has said and done many hurtful things to me. I need your wisdom and guidance in handling these issues. I need your Holy Spirit to provide me a clear path to follow. And, I believe by faith that you will answer this earnest plea. In obedience to you, Lord, I forgive my spouse of sins that [he/she] committed in this relationship. By giving these sins to you, I am releasing this weight from my body, which is your temple. Thank you for allowing me to walk in this liberty. I ask that you touch [spouse's name]'s heart as you are touching my own. I ask these things in the name of Jesus Christ. Amen.

HOW, IF AT ALL, has your spouse disappointed you? Write down up to five of the most significant things your spouse has done to harm you, your marriage, or other people and things that are important to you. After you finish this list, look at it carefully, placing a check next to each one that you have already prayed about and forgiven. Now, place an *X* next to each one that remains unforgiven. How does it make you feel to see what is checked and what is not? God desires you to forgive any of these *X*'s today.

The Fourth Movement: Redeeming Your Spouse

As you have offered and received forgiveness in steps one, two, and three, you have invited the divine intercession of the Holy Spirit into your marriage. Jesus says that where there is light, darkness cannot exist. Whether or not you feel it or see it, your acts of contrition are moving the Lord's hand on your behalf. By engaging in these steps, you have proven yourself obedient. The final step in climbing the redemptive stone in your marriage is redeeming your partner. Forgiveness is a necessary precursor to redemption. Think of Jesus' plea for humanity even as he agonized on Calvary. Jesus cried for you and for me, "Father, forgive them; for they do not know what they are doing" (Luke 23:34, NRSV). By offering forgiveness, Jesus creates the context for redemption.

Your own acts of forgiveness have created space for redemption in your marriage. Rather than trying to convince your partner of the errors of his or her ways or withdrawing into silent suffering, you have chosen a more righteous path. But this is only the beginning. Your heart is now fertile ground for providing redemptive covering for your spouse.

After Adam and Eve's disobedience noted in the third chapter of Genesis (3:21), God provides a temporary covering, animal skins, for them to hide their nakedness—nakedness about which they were formerly unashamed. How many of our marriages are covered with temporary covering due to our own sinfulness? God is calling your relationship with your spouse to be without shame. The Holy Spirit has equipped you to invoke his power. It is unrealistic to believe that you will no longer make mistakes in your marriage. But, the blood of the Lamb covers your missteps as you continue to submit your efforts to God.

Spousal Redemption: To Petition

What does it mean, practically, to redeem or cover your spouse? Redeeming your spouse is a two-step process of petitioning and protecting that is built upon the cornerstone of marriage: agape love. First, let us consider petitioning. You can petition for your spouse before God and before others through prayer. No person is in a better position to recognize your spouse's prayer needs than you. You know his successes and failures; her highs and lows. When you petition before God on your spouse's behalf, you pray for strength and increased faith in difficult circumstances. Even when your partner is too frustrated, dejected, or angry to pray, you provide the covering. When confidence is shaken, egos are hurt, or fortitude wavers, your petitions to God protect.

I am reminded of instances in my marriage where my wife's confidence and belief in me was voiced in our prayer time together. Not only did God meet my psychological needs, but hearing my wife approach God on my behalf was therapeutic in itself. It is no wonder that Jesus says, "If two of you agree on earth about anything you ask, it will be done for you by my Father in heaven" (Matthew 18:19, NRSV). While it is ideal that you and your partner have prayer time together to intercede on each other's behalf, do not let unavailability or disinterest dissuade you. Satan does not easily concede territory. Remember Scripture's caveat that some things only come through prayer and fasting. You can petition on your spouse's behalf with or without his or her knowledge. Believe that, in time, your spouse will be your partner in prayer.

Your petitions for your spouse can also be made among people in your circle of influence. When you show verbal and nonverbal support for your spouse's weaknesses and encouragement of his or her strengths before your children, friends, family, peers, and church members, you are petitioning on his or her behalf. Your words of covering accentuate your spouse's sense of spiritual, emotional, and psychological health and provide energy to become all that God has purposed him or her to be. However, you are only able to provide this type of covering as you listen with ears and heart to understand. Your spouse will only expose his or her vulnerability to you as you demonstrate yourself to be trustworthy as his or her protector.

Spousal Redemption: To Protect

The second aspect of covering your spouse is protection. Just as the Lord is the protector to those who trust in his wings, you are to be your spouse's protector. You are best positioned to know your spouse's heart and empathize with his or her struggles. Rather than exposing your spouse to others, your duty is to work with her to improve herself (if she is receptive to this act). Redeeming your spouse means that you cover his emotional vulnerabilities. Remember, protecting your spouse does not mean that you make excuses for his errant behavior. God does not expect you to be party to ungodly behaviors. You are never expected to lie, steal, or otherwise sin to hide your spouse's guilt. In some instances, exposing your spouse's guilt appropriately is, in fact, offering protection. If your spouse needs to be protected from him- or herself, such behavior is often warranted. Ordeals involving substance abuse and addictions are typical instances in which protecting your spouse may warrant revealing your loved one to organizations that can aid in his or her recovery.

Let us review the four essential steps to climbing the redemptive stone in your marriage. First, repent to God for your mistakes in the marriage. Second, repent to your spouse for your role in the marriage's falling short of God's will. Third, forgive your spouse for his or her mistakes. And, fourth, redeem or cover your spouse through petitioning and protection. It is easy to think of these steps as a linear climb in which each step clearly follows the previous one. In actuality, this climb toward redemption is a painstaking back-and-forth process of triumphs and miscues. The decision to climb the redemptive stone in your marriage is a decision to believe the promise of God rather than the troubles that have historically rocked your marriage. As you engage these four steps, I believe that your spouse will feel the unconditional love of Christ in your marriage.

We began the last chapter with the timeless story of David's triumph over the giant Goliath. On its face, this battle seemed lopsided, with lots cast against the undersized and under-armed shepherd. Your marriage may also feel like a hopeless uphill battle in which everyone considers you down for the count. I remind you that the battle is not yours, nor is it just about you. The battle for your marriage impacts people across generations you may never meet in this lifetime. Your marriage is God's battle.

I ROCK Exercises

Scripture Memorization: John 20:23

If you forgive anyone his sins, they are forgiven; if you do not forgive them, they are not forgiven.

Contemplation

Respond to the following points of contemplation in your personal journal:

1. In what areas of your life do you need more prayer support? Why are your spouse's prayers so important to you in this area? What is the best way to communicate your needs to your spouse so that your concerns are understood?
2. We all need to feel safe and protected. When do you most need your spouse's protection?
3. How will your spouse's covering in these areas impact your life and marriage?

Integration

4. Find or write a song to play for your spouse that best summarizes the spiritual, psychological, or physical aspects of "covering" that you need from him or her.

We ROCK Exercises

Contemplation

1. The title of this chapter is "Exchange Guilt for Grace." How guilt-free is your marriage? Talk about what impact a guilt-free marriage might have on your family.

Integration

2. Share the letters that you have written in this chapter requesting and offering forgiveness from your spouse.
3. Play or sing the songs that you chose and explain why you chose them.

PART THREE

Discovering Offering: The Rock of Sacrifice

A great marriage is not when the 'perfect couple' come together.
It is when an imperfect couple learns to enjoy their differences.
—Dave Meurer

Offering

Marriage ROCKS is about the role of God in your marriage. In earlier chapters, you reflected on your own strengths and weakness in the relationship. Prayerfully, you have seen how Christ's sacrifice for your sins models the level of commitment God desires you to have toward your marriage. As you and your spouse continue to work towards being redemptive to each other, you are in prime position to take the next step towards authentic marriage. This step, which is known as Offering, is the foundation for intimacy with God and with your spouse. We examine the story of an unlikely biblical hero called Gideon to understand how God shows approval of that which you offer to him and by association in your marriage.

When the angel of the LORD appeared to Gideon, he said, "The LORD is with you, mighty warrior."

"But sir," Gideon replied, "if the LORD is with us, why has all this happened to us? Where are all his wonders that our fathers told us about when they said, 'Did not the LORD bring us up out of Egypt?' But now the LORD has abandoned us and put us into the hand of Midian."

Then the LORD turned to him and said, "Go in the strength you have and save Israel out of Midian's hand. Am I not sending you?"

"But Lord," Gideon asked, "how can I save Israel? My clan is the weakest in Manasseh, and I am the least in my family!"

The Lord answered, "I will be with you, and you will strike down all the Midianites together." Gideon replied, "If now I have found favor in your eyes, give me a sign that it is really you talking to me. Please do not go away until I come back and bring my offering and set it before you."

And the LORD said, "I will wait until you return."

Gideon went in, prepared a young goat, and from an ephah of flour he made bread without yeast. Putting the meat in a basket and its broth in a pot, he brought them out and offered them to him under the oak.

The angel of God said to him, "Take the meat and the unleavened bread, place them on this rock, and pour out the broth." And Gideon did so. With the tip of the staff that was in his hand, the angel of the LORD touched the meat and the unleavened bread. Fire flared from the rock, consuming the meat and the bread. And the angel of the LORD disappeared (Judges 6:12-21).

CHAPTER 6

Step 3: Present an Acceptable Offering

And every priest stands day after day at his service,
offering again and again the same sacrifices that can never
take away sins. But when Christ had offered for all time a
single sacrifice for sins, "he sat down at the right hand of God,"
and since then has been waiting "until his enemies would
be made a footstool for his feet." For by a single offering
he has perfected for all time those who are sanctified.
—Hebrews 10:11-14, NRSV

Offering: Something Presented for Acceptance

As African American Christians, we are familiar with the term
offering. At every Sunday service, we participate in the collection
of offerings. Such familiarity, however, often causes us to lose the
spiritual significance of the offering. In order to fully comprehend
God's perspective in marriage, we need to consider offering from
God's vantage point (or at least as close to it as we can manage).
The offering system was dictated by God to draw his people to
him, and within African American marriages, to bring us closer to
God and each other. Herein lies the ultimate achievement of intimacy with God and in marriage. We will use the story of Gideon
as a launching pad for this next leg of this journey toward authentic marriage.

David's conquest of Goliath took place circa 1100 BC and sig-
nified a major power shift in the military domination of the
Hebrew nation during David's reign. Previously, the Hebrew
military was governed by God-appointed judges. During this

period, the Hebrew people weakened in their commitment to the ways of God, resulting in a three-hundred-year cycle of sin, captivity, repentance, and restoration. This is when the story of Gideon occurs. This story introduces us to the second marriage rock: offering.

In contrast to the confidence and exuberance shown by David in wielding the redemptive stone, Gideon's story speaks to the frailty and insecurity of our Christian walk.

> **HAVE YOU EVER** felt weak and insecure in your marriage? Those who have can probably relate to Gideon's position. Write down any occasions in your marriage when you felt such insecurity. How, if at all, were you able to move beyond these emotions?

Gideon's rise as a judge of the nation of Israel is another powerful example of how God can transform a person of weak faith into a model of leadership. Even more astounding is the grace God shows in raising up a deliverer out of a family steeped in idolatry. Gideon's cry to God in Judges 6 resonates for those married folks who also cry out to the Lord, "If you are with us, why has all of this happened to us?" Just like Gideon, you too may be waiting to see God perform miracles in the midst of your marital struggles.

The keys to Gideon's faith development were acts of sacrifice and offering. Therefore, if you are not using the waiting period as a time of preparation (through sacrifice and offering), you may be waiting a long time for God to answer your cries.

The term *offering* is commonly used in Christian circles. However, the chapters in Part 3 challenge you to think deeply and systematically about offering—a process guaranteed to enhance your marriage relationship. Slowly read Gideon's vignette again. I encourage you to read the entire sixth chapter of Judges in order to understand the larger context of what was happening with the Hebrew nation and with Gideon more particularly. What themes stand out? Are there aspects of this story that resonate with your own personal experiences?

When I consider the story of Gideon, I think about the call of God. I see Gideon's rock—the rock that consumed the offering—as a powerful symbol of sacrifice. I speak not only of physical sacrifice. Gideon's sacrifice was also emotional, in that it challenged the very fabric of Gideon's lifestyle. Earlier in Judges 6, God challenges Gideon to leave his comfort zone by tearing down his father's idols, an act that brought public scorn upon him. God further insists that Gideon reconsider his self-worth and value to his community. Few offerings are more costly than the emotional ones, but these are the ones we must be willing to sacrifice in marital work.

Understanding Sacrifice and Offering

By claiming the first stone, the redemptive stone, in Part 2, you made the decision (giving and receiving forgiveness) necessary for covering your marriage with the love of Christ. Forgiveness and agape love are building blocks upon which your marriage will elevate to the next plateau: offering. I call this second step *offering* because it is the essence of sacrifice. Phrased another way, within the kingdom of God, sacrifice precedes offering. Let's examine these terms, *sacrifice* and *offering*, more carefully.

A Lesson on Sacrifice

Sacrifice means to give up something valuable to you. It sounds inherently noble, but this is a gravely incorrect assumption that can foster misunderstanding in marriages. Sacrifice is sometimes done only for the benefit of another—but this is not always true.

Simply put, sacrifice can be unselfish, such as a spouse who gives up a rewarding and successful career in order to be home with the children. It can also be selfish, such as the spouse who gives up a favorite hobby in order to further his or her own ego-driven career goals. These somewhat simple examples highlight two important aspects of sacrifice. First, sacrifice can be either self-centered (all or mostly about you) or other-centered (all or mostly about someone else). The second attribute of sacrifice is that it has two dimensions: external (the natural or physical) and internal (the psychological and spiritual).

Examine closely what the parent described above is ultimately sacrificing. The job may be a source of emotional (if not intellectual and financial) fulfillment. From an external perspective, this person may be sacrificing benefits he or she relishes, such as financial flexibility and rewarding relationships with coworkers. Comprehending the internal perspective requires understanding the emotional and spiritual meaning of the job. Intrinsically, the job may offer a sense of belonging, heightened self-worth, or working for some transcendent good.

Without this broader perspective, individual spouses and marriages may fail to fully grasp the extent to which one is impacted by the individual sacrifices of another. Consider a simple example outside of the marriage context. Parents routinely sacrifice their own desires and even needs for the benefit of their children. But children are often blind to the extent of their parents' sacrifice. While we accept this lack of appreciation between parents and children, marriage is an entirely different matter. In marriage, these unacknowledged emotions and disappointments can corrode the balance of trust and respect in the marriage for years to come. The story of Wayne and Latonya illustrates this.

Wayne and Latonya, a young couple with one child and another on the way, are struggling in their six-year marriage. Wayne wants Latonya to stay home with their two children after the baby is born. Wayne has wanted Latonya to stay home since their first child, Kenyon, was born. Latonya, however, enjoys her job as a public defender working on behalf of mostly disenfranchised communities. Wayne feels strongly that the kids' lives will be better with Latonya staying home with them. He has tried appealing to her analytically, emotionally, and financially. But, Latonya insists that the children will be fine if she continues to work. She is beginning to resent Wayne's insistence otherwise. During most of this current pregnancy, Latonya has complained that she agreed to have another child only after Wayne agreed that her career would not be jeopardized. She feels betrayed by Wayne and believes he does not appreciate her sacrifice.

So, how can Wayne and Latonya use this lesson of sacrifice to overcome this difficult time in their marriage? As in most such cases, it begins with communication. Wayne and Latonya have become entrenched in their respective positions, both with valid reasons for feeling the way they do. They are talking at each other. But, they are failing to communicate the emotions behind their positions. Wayne does not appear to appreciate fully what Latonya's career means to her. His attempts to coerce her through logic and guilt are actually destroying their marriage. What might happen if Wayne first uses empathy to share with Latonya the value that he sees in the way she balances what she does on her job and her responsibilities at home? How might this be enhanced if Wayne follows this genuine appreciation for the good that he sees in Latonya's efforts with a question to better understand her sacrifice such as "what feeling is strongest when I mention to you my desire for you to resign from your job to care for the children?" Finally, Wayne needs to listen carefully for the emotion that Latonya shares to fully grasp her point of view.

For her part, Latonya needs to explore why it is so important to Wayne that she stay home. She too needs to take an empathic stance to understand the emotions behind Wayne's perspective. What does he fear will happen to the children if Latonya continues working? If Wayne and Latonya can change their stance from enemies to allies on this topic, they may be able to negotiate an arrangement that addresses the emotional needs they both have.

When you are on the listening side of such a conversation, check your defenses and be curious about what your partner is sharing. Your partner's sense of sacrifice is valid, whether or not you get it. As Wayne and Latonya seek understanding, they will be in a better position to hear how God wants to use this specific situation to bring them closer together.

> **Authentic marriage is above all a commitment to prioritizing God's will for your marriage above your own. Your marriage represents sacrifice— a means of drawing you closer to God.**

As explained by Rabbi Shmuel Silinsky, the Hebrew word for sacrifice, *korban*, comes from the root *korav*, meaning "to come close," clearly connoting the intent that sacrifice brings the giver close to God. Rabbi Silinsky continues, "The offering was meant to bring someone who was far near once again."[1] In our sinful state, we are far removed from God. Through the sacrifice of Christ, we who call him Savior come close to the Lord. As you come to the Lord, you are spiritually and psychologically empowered to come closer to your spouse. Authentic marriage is above all a commitment to prioritizing God's will for your marriage above your own. Your marriage represents sacrifice—a means of drawing you closer to God.

A Lesson on Offering

Now that we understand *sacrifice,* we can consider *offering.* An offering is a presentation made by one to another. The presentation can be to a person (such as your spouse), a deity (your God), or an organization (your employer or church). Your offering can be virtually anything. It can be tangible, such as possessions. It can also be intangible, such as your time or your creativity.

Our story of Gideon takes place within the context of specific Old Testament law governing how the Hebrew people were to present offerings to the Lord. In Leviticus, God outlines the different types of offerings and the circumstances in which each offering is either mandated or suggested. The six most commonly mentioned levitical offerings are the burnt offering, the peace offering, the grain offering, the fellowship offering, the sin offering, and the guilt offering. For our purposes, we will use the term *offering* in a general sense.

Although God sanctioned these offerings for different purposes, they all share a common thread: They were intended to communicate humility, obedience, and value in relationships. But, why were offerings needed? Simply put, God's offering system was divinely instituted to solidify Israel's identity as people of God.

When Adam and Eve became aware of their nakedness, they were ashamed. Their human response to this sense of shame was to find a covering—something to hide this sense of shame. They resorted, however, to an unacceptable covering of fig leaves to hide their nakedness. It is God (not Adam or Eve) who sacrifices an animal to provide acceptable clothes to cover the first couple. God's covering of human imperfections has always involved sacrifice— but on God's terms. This is the first time God required offering in order to provide escape from spiritual death and restore humanity to himself. These offerings served to restore the spiritual intimacy between God and humans that was interrupted by sin. This spiritual intimacy can only be restored as we sacrifice our selfish desires in pursuit of God's purposes. In a similar vein, you must heed a similar offering system in order to find spiritual intimacy with your spouse.

We attempt our own temporal offerings to cover our relationship sins. How often have you sought "coverings" in materialism, addictions, self-help books and programs, and even religiosity? These temporary coverings, hoped to foster closeness or distract you from the pain of emotional distance, prove ultimately incapable of protecting the relationship from the difficulties, struggles, and hurts you face. Yet, you may continue to bundle these inadequacies together and offer them to the Lord as your marriage. I wonder if it may be that God is rejecting the offering.

Many seek the Lord's blessings on marriages that God has already deemed unacceptable, as husbands and wives remain stuck in their own self-centered patterns. The problem is not that God finds you or the person that you married unacceptable. Rather, God questions whether you and your spouse are genuinely sacrificing yourselves. No matter how many prayers you offer, God will never accept your marriage if it is steeped in false coverings, such as greed, destructive habits, or other attempts at self-centered gratification. These false coverings must be discarded to discover the intimacy that God intends. If you are finding that the more you pray to God to heal your marriage, the more you feel overwhelmed by your pain and sin, that may actually be God answering your prayer—by putting the responsibility right back on you to check your own motives and sacrifices.

Let us revisit our example of Wayne and Latonya. How can they make offerings to one another to resolve this marital conflict? If Wayne took the suggestion to empathize with Latonya's sacrifice, he might feel compelled to consider changes to his own job, so that he can be home more with the children. Latonya would likely be moved by Wayne's offering because it validates his concern for her needs and it honors the promise that he made earlier that she would not have to leave her job. Such a move increases her trust in him. Alternatively, perhaps Latonya could cut her schedule back and work less or look into working from home. Her offering would be found acceptable to Wayne because it shows concern for his worries about the welfare of their children. There are many examples of acceptable offerings this couple can make. The key for Wayne and Latonya—and for your own marriage—is acceptability, as couples seek to satisfy mutual needs. In order to understand your partner's sacrifice, you need to honestly discuss the meaning behind the sacrifice.

What is gained by these offerings? Each demonstrates a move away from selfishness—a willingness to leave something behind that is important. Each prioritizes the spouse's desires and needs over his or her own preferences. Each offering would be a decision to leave the comfort zone and offer grace to the other. These are the components of an acceptable offering to each other and to God because they convey the message of servanthood. Servanthood is not a term we often think of in the context of marriage. But, every act of service to your spouse is an offering that God honors—even if sometimes your spouse does not see it that way. At the basic level, each would offer a commitment to leaving, cleaving, and becoming one—to covenant.

In reality, every act of covenant in marriage is an act of obedience to God. The covenant commitment that is offered comes at a price. This is, however, what makes the offering so meaningful to the Lord. It is like King David when he says to Araunah, "No, I insist on paying you for it. I will not sacrifice to the LORD my God burnt offerings that cost me nothing" (2 Samuel 24:24, NIV). Regardless of your spouse's acceptance or rejection of this covenant commitment, God finds your offering acceptable.

Interdependence of Sacrifice and Offering

You determine the value of your sacrifice, but the same does not apply for offering. Regardless of the nature of your offering, it will be accepted or rejected based on its value to the recipient. Think about this: No matter how priceless your offering is to you, if it means nothing to the person to whom it is being given, then that person will physically or psychologically reject the offering.

What does this mean for your marriage? The key centers upon the acceptability of your offering to the Lord—a measure directly connected to the quality of your sacrifice. When beholden to a God-centered model, offering and sacrifice are interdependent. One's offering can never be fully comprehended without understanding one's sacrifice. How can we comprehend the offering that Wayne wants Latonya to make unless we grasp how much she would sacrifice to accommodate his request? Sacrifice and offering are connected.

We sacrifice for our marriages. But, if sacrifice is relinquishing that which is important to you, how much of your sacrifice is truly done for your spouse? There are some useful examples of sacrifice and offering being integrated in the Old Testament (e.g., Cain and Abel's offerings in Genesis 4) and in the New Testament (e.g., Christ's death for the sins of humanity).

The primary point to fathom, however, is that the Old Testament model of sacrifice and offering of animals and crops shifts to the New Testament focus on giving up oneself as sacrifice. But, God's purpose for sacrifice and offering has always remained the same: to provide a bridge to connect us intimately with the Lord. Underline the word *intimately*.

In this same vein, the God-centered offerings we present to others, including our spouses, are also bridges to intimacy. You may wonder, "But what if my spouse does not accept my offering?" Remember, Christ's offering of innocent blood was not contingent upon acceptance by humanity but by God. While your spouse may consider your offering worthless and unacceptable, God accepts your earnest offering as priceless—a bridge to a more intimate relationship with him and, prayerfully, with your spouse.

I ROCK Exercises

Scripture Memorization: 2 Samuel 24:24, NIV

But the king [David] replied to Araunah, "No, I insist on paying you for it. I will not sacrifice to the LORD my God burnt offerings that cost me nothing." So David bought the threshing floor and the oxen and paid fifty shekels of silver for them.

Contemplation

Respond to the following points of contemplation in your personal journal:

1. Contrast the confidence of David in the Part 2 opener with the frailty of Gideon in this chapter. What might this difference suggest about the manner in which you approach obstacles in your marriage? Answer this question individually, from your own perspective.
2. What idols have been built in your house that should be torn down in obedience to God? How have you contributed to shaping these idols?
3. Identify the areas in which you believe God has commissioned your marriage. How effectively does Gideon's experience convince you that you already have everything you need to accomplish this? What assets do you recognize that you have? What do you fear you don't have?
4. What failures in your personal and marital life need to be confessed in order to move closer to God?

Integration

5. Jesus told around forty parables that are recorded in the Holy Bible. Find one of the parables that most reminds you of sacrifice and offering in your own marriage. Write in your journal how Jesus' key message pertains to your marriage.

We ROCK Exercises

Contemplation

1. Take your own inventory of the things that you have sacrificed in your marriage. Discuss with your spouse how these sacrifices have affected you physically and emotionally.
2. Discuss with your spouse any instances where you felt your sacrifice and offerings for him or her were underappreciated.
3. What evidence do you desire that would show you that God's hand is upon your marriage? How committed are you to focus on your marriage even if the evidence is not forthcoming?

Integration

4. Sports history is full of real-life stories of people who sacrificed themselves for the greater team good. As a couple, research and find one of these stories that in some way(s) reminds you of sacrifice and offering in your own marriage.

CHAPTER 7

Step 4: Enhance Your Intimacy Profile

But if you make for me an altar of stones,
do not build it of hewn stones;
for if you use a chisel upon it you profane it.
—Exodus 20:25, NRSV

The Intimacy Factor

A couple benefits from incorporating the tenets of offering into their relationship because it builds equity in the marriage. The goodwill and trust that builds as partners serve each other form the foundation of healthy marriage. The outgrowth of such a positive exchange is intimacy—spiritual, emotional, and physical.

Most couples fantasize about intimacy. Yet, so many fail to achieve the level of intimacy they desire. In too many instances, such difficulties often lead to fragmented relationships and divorce. Much of this intimacy vacuum is a result of offerings that fail to spark a fire within the marriage because neither person feels understood and loved. I like the Scripture that introduces this chapter because it highlights the importance of reliance upon God to guide one's steps in the marriage. The Lord's instruction here is for his people to avoid interjecting their own expertise and "know-how" when erecting an altar for their offerings. Why? Because, what is often considered wisdom to the human mind only taints or distorts a godly offering. Your job then is to let the Holy Spirit guide what you and your spouse offer to each other in your pursuit of intimacy.

This intimacy pursuit requires that each of you understand the other's intimate needs. For some, intimacy is romantic: it entices, conjuring passionate and seductive images of metaphysical proportions. For others, intimacy is a platonic, non-sexualized emotional tie. Generally, though certainly not always, women tend to be drawn to the emotional aspects of intimacy and desire it as a precursor to sex. Men tend to be opposite; their fantasy lives tend to emphasize the physical aspects of intimacy and from this perspective flows the fostering of emotional bonds. This difference seems to be a great joke from God, as men and women who truly love each other keep missing one another on this point. How do you overcome these differences to find mutually satisfying emotional and sexual intimacy?

During the romantic phase of courtship and early marriage, couples bask in a glow of intimate nirvana (physical and emotional) and relish their time together. Those who are seeking a mate look forward to this intimate romantic relationship. From where does this pursuit of intimacy come? Clearly, it is God-given. The drive toward intimacy is the innate search for one's counterpart. Despite the biological elements fueling our drive for intimate relationships with other humans, an equally fundamental drive is for intimacy with God. God created you with a longing for spiritual discovery—a desire to connect with him. Even atheists and agnostics admit that we have a spiritual compass that points us in the direction of something beyond ourselves.

God has actually wired us for a relational intimacy that is threefold, like the Trinity itself—spiritual, emotional, and sexual. In this chapter, we examine how sacrificial offerings direct you to greater levels of intimacy with both God and your spouse.

Marriage as an Offering

God established the offering system to accomplish a distinct purpose: relational interdependence. The Lord required the Hebrews to offer sacrifices to foster dependence, commitment, and intimacy with him, and the Lord requires the same of your marriage. God's intent for your marriage is that it engenders holiness through spiritual intimacy with God and, by association, with your spouse. In sacrificing your marriage as an offering to God, you are seeking God's acceptance of it, despite the missteps and transgressions that you make along the way. Similar in some ways to redemption, the marital offering acknowledges your compromised state, which renders you unable to fulfill all that God has purposed for you. Offering your marriage to God suggests that you are consecrating yourself to a path of Christ-centered purity.

Building Spiritual Intimacy through Offering

How spiritually intimate is your marriage? It depends on what the phrase *spiritually intimate* means. Some suggest that this refers to sharing the same faith beliefs, avoiding being "unequally yoked." Others believe it means shared devotions and prayer. Still others imagine a metaphysical connectedness with their soul mate. These notions of spiritual intimacy are all legitimate and hold in common a shared space in which a couple can discover God's purpose in them as individuals and as a partnership.

We walk this enlightened path as we offer our prayers to God. Dedication to prayer is, I believe, one contemporary form of offering. I know that when Dalia and I commit ourselves consistently to prayer, we become more interdependent. There was a period in our marriage when Dalia saw my confidence and achievement-oriented resolve, and questioned the degree to which I even needed her. While I was talking about *partner* and *team*, my endless and ambitious pursuits (which I justified as important to the family) failed to integrate Dalia's perspective. During these times, Dalia and I were a committed couple, but we failed to honor God's expectation of marital partnership. As we shifted our focus from commitment to each other to commitment to God's purpose for us, we began to walk a path of spiritual discovery that is still unfolding. Now, I am empowered by the prayers that my wife offers for me. When she petitions the Lord on my behalf, I have come to expect God to do something marvelous. My wife has become my soul mate through the offerings she makes.

God no longer requires that we offer unblemished animal sacrifices to be in relationship with him. In this age, God requires us to offer our unhindered prayers to foster relationship with him. Prayer as offering is not just for marriage; God demands this in general. But, the focus of these prayers (individually or together) is the removal of all stumbling stones that hamper God's will in our marriages.

God intends for prayer to undergird the marital relationship. Be creative about what works for you and your marriage. The state of African American marriages demands this intentional focus. In this season and culture, the nurturing of marriage tends to fall to the bottom of the to-do list; therefore, it is vital that you and your spouse pray more frequently to combat those feelings of inadequacy and hopelessness, and to nurture love and connection.

WHAT DOES spiritual intimacy in marriage mean to you? When a couple is spiritually intimate, what types of things are they doing? As you review your responses, write down examples from your marriage where spiritual intimacy is evident or absent.

Building Emotional Intimacy through Offering

God calls us to emotional and spiritual intimacy, but he leaves to us the decisions regarding the levels of emotional and sexual intimacy we desire. Let's look closer at this important offering. Couples often lament the absence of emotional and sexual intimacy in their marriages. After hours of therapy and scores of self-help books, many couples still feel disconnected beyond the basic interaction required to live together. Even Christian couples, who share a love of God, are dumbfounded by their inability to attain deeper levels of emotional connection and sexual fulfillment.

If you are struggling to achieve this level of intimacy, it may be because you are giving the wrong offerings. If you are offering more possessions, activities, and more social networks, believing that these will rekindle the intimacy flame, your efforts are incomplete.

Offerings lead us to marital health by emphasizing sharing. It is this sharing that creates mutual dependence, which in turn fosters emotional intimacy—a precursor to sexual intimacy. Consider it this way: Offering's emphasis on sharing creates a climate in which emotional and sexual intimacy can develop. If your marriage lacks intimacy, honestly consider these questions:

- Do you try to control things in your marriage? (Are you a control freak?)
- Do you need to win disagreements with your spouse?
- Are you keeping secrets from your spouse?
- Do you have activities, hobbies, or habits that divert your attention from marital challenges?

Issues of domination and control are at the center of these four questions. These power plays are classic intimacy-busters, because selfishness inhibits the climate for sharing. If you responded yes to any of these questions, your marital intimacy will fall short of God's desire. It follows naturally that your sexual relationship with your spouse is not as fulfilling as it can be. Conversely, as you sacrifice yourself in each of these areas, your marital intimacy will increase, but only if you and your spouse commit wholeheartedly to the sacrifice of offerings.

In the last chapter we saw Wayne and Latonya trapped in a stressful pattern where each is trying to control and coerce the other. Rather than appreciating Latonya's concern, Wayne is arguing his position by using guilt to make Latonya feel like a bad mother or showing her the budget to see how much money they will be by spending on childcare. Wayne is being driven by a desire to win the argument in order to get his way. But in order to win, he is counting on making Latonya feel like a loser. This is never a good decision in marriage. You can imagine how this schism impacts their intimacy level.

Latonya is focused on the previous promise that Wayne made to her that she would not have to leave her job if they had another child. She feels betrayed by Wayne's reversal and is allowing these feelings to distance her from Wayne emotionally. In the previous chapter, I suggested that Wayne and Latonya could use empathetic listening to resolve their current impasse over the decision as to whether she resigns from her job to satisfy Wayne's desire for her to care for the children full-time.

Empathic listening boils down to a three-step process. First, it means that you build trust in the relationship by affirming the good and the value in your spouse. Second, it means that you take a nondefensive listening stance that allows you to hear the emotional needs of your partner. Third, empathic listening requires that you look for a solution that satisfies the emotional needs of both parties. These three steps are so important because they tear down barriers of domination and control allowing Wayne and Latonya to really see each other (and their current impasse) in a new way. And, this fresh look is enabled by their willingness to sacrifice their self-serving perspectives for one focused on healing.

> **IN THE PREVIOUS** reflection point, you assessed the spiritual intimacy in your marriage. In what ways has your level of spiritual intimacy affected your emotional intimacy? From your perspective, how connected is spiritual and emotional intimacy in your marriage? Has this always been the same or has it changed over time?

Building Sexual Intimacy through Offering

We recognize sex with our spouse as a right of marriage. While cultural differences nuance its expression, all cultures understand the power of sex. Whether for procreation or pleasure, God designed husbands and wives to embrace sexual expression. In a literal sense, there is no better indication of God's intent that we become one in marriage than the design of our sexual organs. God designed the human body to be shared sexually, and intercourse is intended to be the physical manifestation of spiritual and emotional intimacy. It is a closed feedback loop in which emotional intimacy enhances sexual intimacy, which in turn enhances emotional intimacy. Simply put, without emotional intimacy, you cannot have sexual intimacy.

Of course, this does not mean that it's possible to have sex without emotional intimacy. However, sex and sexual intimacy are not the same things. Many of our Christian marriages have sex at regular (or maybe not-so-regular) intervals, but the sex feels unfulfilling. Sex has become routine, boring, and, in some distraught marriages, even annoying. Do you wonder where the pizzazz and romance are? While this question may periodically surface in everyone's marriage, if this is a question on which you think often, stop ignoring it. This question often leads spouses to doubt whether they are in love with or are loved by their spouse at all. This doubt can create an atmosphere that makes it more likely that one or both partners will find emotional or sexual fulfillment outside of the marriage.

Sex-related concerns are one of the top three problem issues of marriage. Sexual incompatibility is increasingly identified as a credible reason to divorce. (There is that word again—*incompatibility*.) This raises two questions: Why is sex such a divisive issue? And, how can sex be transformed from an issue of conflict into a source of emotional connection? The divisiveness surrounding sex centers upon two dynamics.

The first dynamic involves the struggle to compensate for differences in how men and women are sexually aroused and satisfied. This requires communication around biological differences in the sexual-response cycle. Sexual intimacy requires you to understand what arouses your spouse.

The second concerns unrealistic expectations of what a meaningful sexual encounter looks and feels like, fueled by rampant misperceptions surrounding what constitutes good sex. From the embellished stories of teenagers to the scripted encounters on screen, our lives are filled with sex talk. In the media, sex is rarely cast in the context of a healthy, monogamous, married relationship. Instead, sex is depicted as readily available with whoever is around, and it is always fantastic. Movies portray wives who raise children, work full-time, cook gourmet meals, clean meticulously, and anticipate passionate, erotic sex with their husbands—all in a day's work.

Television couplings do not have sexual dysfunction or premature ejaculation. We watch women turn from being angry at the male to sexually aroused within the span of two minutes. I am sure that the absurdity of these portrayals is clear to anyone who is married. Yet, to an alarming degree, these lies invade our consciousness and make us wonder why our real-life sexual encounters lack the passion of their media counterparts. I have created a term for this Satan-induced distortion of sexual intimacy: *sextimacy*.

God's design for sex is not simply the act of physical union but an expression of sharing the innermost part of ourselves. Sextimacy, however, is false intimacy with limited ability to unite a couple; it is sexuality without spiritual and emotional offerings. Many individuals engage in sex and intentionally disconnect from any emotional baggage that could foster a sense of commitment. Many married couples also view sex as more of an obligation than the divine experience that God intended it to be. God desires to replace sextimacy with authentic sexuality built upon offering— sharing yourselves openly and unashamedly.

Authentic sexuality is insight that understands your erogenous zones as well as the emotional context they exist to serve. Authentic sexuality seeks to pleasure your spouse as much as pleasuring yourself. And, authentic sexuality is encouragement that you are loved, whether sexual expression is ideal or whether there are missteps and miscues.

I ROCK Exercises

Scripture Memorization: Exodus 20:25, NRSV

But if you make for me an altar of stones, do not build it of hewn stones; for if you use a chisel upon it you profane it.

Contemplation

Respond to the following points of contemplation in your personal journal:
1. How important is it to you to be spiritually intimate with your partner? How spiritually intimate is your marriage currently? What prevents spiritual intimacy in your marriage?
2. How fulfilling is the emotional intimacy in your marriage? Does your spouse feel differently?

3. Domination and control account for many of the intimacy lapses in marriage. How might these issues be influencing the emotional intimacy in your marriage?

Integration

4. Emotional intimacy means different things to different people. Develop your own perspective on emotional intimacy by making a collage of pictures (at least five) that you cull from magazines, newspapers, or other sources that visually communicate what emotional intimacy means to you.

We ROCK Exercises

Contemplation

1. As a couple, it is time for sex talk. Discuss how fulfilling each of you perceives your sexual intimacy to be. What might make your sexual relationship better?
2. This chapter talks about false sexual intimacy. Discuss ways you and your spouse allow sextimacy to disrupt your authentic sexual intimacy. How might you overcome this false sexual expression?

Integration

3. As a couple, watch the classic 1940 film *The Philadelphia Story*. After watching the movie, discuss how this movie speaks to the shortcomings in your marriage. What hopes and desires does this movie communicate to you about your own marriage? How does it influence your own thoughts of sacrifice and offering?

CHAPTER 8

Step 5: Make TIME for Intimacy

I'm certain that most couples
expect to find intimacy in marriage,
but somehow it eludes them.
–DR. JAMES C. DOBSON

Meeting Needs Takes Time

Marital offerings foster interdependence between spouses by prioritizing the other's needs over one's own. This interdependent pursuit of intimacy is a long-term investment that develops only as couples intentionally make time to share their lives.

Sharing time conveys priority. Because you choose what to do with your time, you make a statement about your marital relationship when you prioritize it over other activities. Gender differences, however, often make sharing time difficult. Husbands tend to view spending time together as functional. The typical male might ask, "What will we do during this time?" Wives, however, see sharing time as relational: "How important am I to him?" As we discuss intimacy, I would like to introduce you to Alan and Vicky. As you read their story in the sidebar, ask yourself how your time commitment to marriage compares to theirs.

Alan and Vicky, a midlife African American couple, have been married almost twenty years; yet, their lives have been on parallel tracks for much of this time. While they have some good memories as parents of three children, they spent little time thinking about their marriage until a year ago. Up to that point, when Alan wasn't working his full-time job, he spent his free time in real estate—buying fixer-uppers and flipping them for a profit. After Vicky's day job was done, all her energies turned toward the children. When Alan and Vicky spent time together outside of the occasional sexual interlude, it was nearly always related to something they had to do for the kids.

Everything changed last year after Alan was badly injured when he fell from a ladder while repairing one of his properties. Vicky, his caregiver during his recovery, realized for the first time that, although she loved Alan, she felt distant from him. She tried talking to him about this, but Alan felt that things were fine. When he tried to appease Vicky's concerns by suggesting they get a babysitter and go out dancing or to a movie (his favorite activities), she seemed distant. His attempt to create closeness by purchasing the diamond necklace she had been wanting was equally unsuccessful.

Although he won't admit it, Alan is confused and angry about what he perceives to be Vicky's childish behavior. Vicky is becoming increasingly depressed about the direction of their marriage. She is frustrated that from her perspective Alan seems unwilling to do anything about it.

An acceptable offering requires that you take your spouse's desires into account (just as a giver would with God). Husbands and wives, however, struggle to put themselves into the shoes of the other. Classic research by Dr. Willard Harley gives us insight into how the differing needs of husbands and wives render empathy difficult.[1] More recently in research with over seven hundred couples, Gary and Barbara Rosberg affirm how much of the struggle to be sensitive to the needs of the other boils down to the differences in husbands' and wives' love needs.[2]

It is important, however, to realize that ultimately Alan and Vicky's disconnect, and the frustrations that you experience with your spouse, are not about research or statistics. In fact, in your marriage the needs discussed above may be reversed entirely. Ultimately, the acceptability in your offering boils down to the needs of two people, you and your spouse. Your growth as a couple is about what each of you brings to the altar as individuals. Your emotional connection centers on your ability to understand and communicate to the heart of your spouse.

The individual nature of offering should not surprise us because it is the way of Scripture. God examines our hearts individually. Our pursuit of salvation is individual. And, ultimately our heavenly reward will be intimately personal.

Adam and Vicky face the same challenge that so many of our marriages face—finding time for true intimacy. Alan and Vicky need to spend time rebuilding the foundation of their marriage. The troubled foundation of their marriage has been masked for years by a veneer of activities. Can you relate to this? For all of us, it is only a matter of time before a veneer tarnishes. Alan needs to hear Vicky's pleas for conversation and understanding.

Since husbands and wives often express basic needs differently, and since individual wants vary greatly, you may have to stretch beyond your comfort zone to join empathically with your spouse. If your spouse's needs orient toward affection and conversation, your marital intimacy may benefit from something as "meaningless" as spending time together in the kitchen during meal preparation. If, however, your spouse's intimacy needs are more physical in nature (e.g., sexual fulfillment and recreational companionship) you need a game plan to spend quality time meeting those physical needs such as recreational companionship and more intimate sexual relations. Meeting one another's needs is about spending time together with intentional focus.

By offering time that is acceptable to your spouse, you are fulfilling his or her most fundamental needs in the marriage. This investment erects standing stones of trust and respect, standing stones that are prerequisites for an acceptable offering and intimacy. It is no different than your relationship with God. Just as it is absurd to believe that giving more monetary gifts to God's work somehow enhances your spiritual intimacy with the Lord, it is equally fallacious to hope to purchase intimacy with your spouse. This is a lesson that could have saved Alan several thousand dollars. What they both really need is free yet priceless. How would you counsel Alan and Vicky?

Discovering the TIME for Intimacy

When thinking about offering time, it is natural to limit our thinking to chronological time. However, any given minute, hour, or day obviously falls short of our mandate. In pre-Socratic times, Greek mythology recognized Chronos as the personification of time—typically portrayed as an old man with a long gray beard. Many associate this fabled character with the name "Father Time." This cultural fable speaks to our own needs to bring time to life in our own marriages. In our daily grind of bills, chores, jobs, and children, we lose the meaning and potential of each day. It takes a serious illness or death to give us momentary pause to reflect. But, this introspection quickly fades as the pressures to resume our harried lives weigh on us. How do we make time more human and personal? In what ways might we learn intimacy with each other by personifying time?

It is with these questions in mind that I conceptualize TIME as an acronym for *touch, insight, mutuality,* and *encouragement.* Each of these aspects necessitates spending meaningful amounts of chronological time together. In total, they give a robust sense of the postures and behaviors that foster emotional intimacy, if they are offered in an acceptable manner. Building emotional intimacy requires the offering of TIME.

Offering Touch

The first TIME element that spouses must offer as they seek to build emotional intimacy is touch. Experimental psychology and neuroscience have long noted that touch triggers the release of chemicals in the brain called *endorphins*, a God-given analgesic that is more powerful than heroin or morphine. Touch also increases levels of melatonin and the feel-good hormone, sero-tonin. Research has shown that touch promotes faster growth in premature babies, reduces pain, decreases autoimmune disease symptoms, lowers glucose levels in children with diabetes, and improves immune systems in people with cancer.[3]

Jesus and the Power of Touch

Medical research finally appears to be catching up with what Scripture recognized long ago. Christ himself used touch to heal. Jesus touched the man with leprosy (Matthew 8:3; Mark 1:41), the eyes of the blind man at Bethsaida (Mark 8:22-25), and the ear and tongue of the man who was blind and deaf (Mark 7:33-35). Why did Jesus touch them when he could have simply spoken the words, as he did for other miracles?

One brain study found that when women simply touched the hands of their husbands, there was an instant drop in activity in the areas of the women's brains involved in fear, danger, and threat. The level of the drop varied, depending on the self-reported quality of the marriage. In other words, women in the strongest marriages felt safer when holding the hands of their husbands as compared to women who described their marriages as less nour-ishing. Other research clearly shows that touch nonverbally com-municates emotions. Touch can reliably communicate love, gratitude, and sympathy, perhaps even more effectively than facial expressions. Of course, touch can also be used to convey negative emotions such as anger and fear.[4]

How important is touch in your own marriage? If you and your spouse struggle with intimacy issues, touch deficits may play a role. Are you happy with the amount of touch in your marriage? What about your partner? Your perspectives may differ widely based on gender and personality differences, and this means that communication is even more important.

Sexualized and Nonsexualized Touch

Husbands frequently sexualize touch, believing (more like hoping) it may be a precursor to sexual arousal and, ultimately, intercourse.

Wives tend to have a longer progression to sexual arousal, so brief moments of touch are unlikely to evoke such a sexualized response. For husbands, one key to building emotional intimacy with our wives is to suppress our desire to turn all meaningful touch into sex. Here is an example from my own marriage. One area that has been a struggle for me is my wife's desire to cuddle together. I learned over time that for Dalia, cuddling does not mean that a sexual encounter is imminent (much to my initial disappointment, I might add). Therefore, there was a point in our marriage where I questioned the purpose of cuddling, if it was not leading to sex. Without the promise of sex, cuddling lacked what I considered a good cost-benefit ratio according to my own "productivity" drive.

As I have become more aware of Dalia's desire and less driven by my own self-centered libido, I am better able to appreciate the benefit of the emotional capital created during these times of cuddling. Although there is certainly a place for the progression of touch to sexual intimacy, we husbands must be able to master the use of touch to emotionally connect with our spouses. I suspect that, if Alan is able to get beyond his search for quick and easy solutions to Vicky's frustration, and if he holds her physically close, some of the relational warmth may return.

The message to wives is also clear. The touching moments that you allow to build into authentic sexual encounters will foster emotional connections with your husband. While there will be times when you do not want touch to lead to sex, keep in mind that your husband may be inclined to perceive your occasional lack of motivation as a personal rejection. It is important to find ways to communicate that your disinterest in sex does not mean disinterest in him. Vicky should take note of this advice. She has been so upset with Alan's lack of sensitivity to her needs that she has disregarded his sexual advances as self-centered.

A Healing Elixir

The hope for this touch offering is that by sacrificing your own touch needs and preferences in favor of those of your spouse, you make an offering that honors God, blesses your spouse, and benefits you, too. Following Jesus' example, your touch can metaphorically heal emotional blindness and deafness in your marriage.

Recently, I discovered a touch secret worth sharing. Every morning when Dalia and I pray, I actually place my arm around her or hold her hand. I find that this simple touch act psychologically releases any negative thoughts I may have about something Dalia has done or said. In a few instances, I have had to force myself to do this because I wanted to be mad at her. But, by pushing through this resistance to place my arm around her, the time of prayer reproved me for my blindness and reinforced in me the joy of having Dalia as my wife.

In developing this chapter, I did something that I had never done before. I asked Dalia what, if anything, it meant to her that I put my arm around her during our prayer times. Her answer warmed my heart. She said that holding her in this way gives her a sense of closeness and warmth. Dalia recalled one instance when we were in disagreement before our prayer time: "I knew at once you were upset with me. And, if you had not held me during the prayer, the disagreement between us would have probably escalated. But, by holding me, you bridged the gap." I love the *bridge the gap* phrase that Dalia used here. Touch is an emotional bridge to intimacy.

Building emotional intimacy takes a commitment to physical touch in your marriage, especially if at least one spouse's love language is touch. The following touch tips promise to improve the emotional intimacy in your marriage when you offer your best in a spirit of selflessness, authenticity, and love—requisite attributes for an offering to be considered *first fruit* in Scripture:

1. Hold hands when you pray together.
2. Give your spouse a loving touch after a conflict.
3. Give your spouse a massage when stress is evident.
4. Hug your spouse for thirty seconds when either of you is feeling discouraged.
5. Cuddle for fifteen minutes without any distractions (e.g., television, kids) at least once per week.

Offering Insight

The second TIME element that spouses must offer as they seek to build emotional intimacy is insight—or understanding the underlying truth. How might Alan and Vicky gain insight in their current marital friction? Understanding underlying truth entails observing your spouse curiously for clues as to his or her motivation and intention. Further and critically, it requires communicating your observations and questions effectively.

Insight Considers Motivation

Authentically understanding another's motivation means that you appreciate the intensity of two fundamental drives: desires and fears. Desire-driven motivation captures one's aspirations, dreams, and longings. Fear-driven motivation encompasses actual or perceived threats that may be unconscious or conscious. Assessing the intensity of these desires and fears provides the clues to understanding motivation.

Let's consider a simple example of motivation using Alan and Vicky's current troubles. Alan is frustrated with Vicky's repeated refusal to accompany him to the movies or dancing. On the surface, Alan may be tempted to interpret Vicky's refusal as a personal rejection or as prioritizing her own self-centered desires over spending time doing something he enjoys. Yes, Vicky may be rejecting him. It is possible that she is being selfish. But, it is also possible that neither interpretation is valid.

If someone can help Alan understand the motivation behind Vicky's refusal, he might discover that she feels scared that her marriage is disintegrating, because she feels lonely and unimportant to Alan. The point here is that, until he understands this fear, he will respond based on superficial rather than authentic understanding. Although her motivation may not be conscious, it nevertheless impacts her.

Many partners fail to respond appropriately to unconscious motivations, because they don't believe they're "real." How could Alan respond in a way that increases the possibility of truly understanding Vicky's motivation? Keep this in mind: The centerpiece of insight is active listening.

**Discovering your spouse's motivations necessitates
listening for verbal and nonverbal expressions
of emotions, needs, hurts, and fears.**

We are all accustomed to listening with our ears. Active listening, however, implies more; it is "listening" with your full sensory capacity, including emotional intuition. Discovering your spouse's motivations necessitates listening for verbal and nonverbal expressions of emotions, needs, hurts, and fears. Alan needs to approach his wife first with his feelings of disappointment, frustration, and hurt when she rebuffs his attempts to connect. He could affirm his love for her regardless of whether or not she goes with him, and could emphasize his desire to understand her reservations. By actively listening and probing, he may uncover the fear underneath her behavior. This active listening process may even help Vicky better understand herself.

Fear is a powerful yet under appreciated motivator. Whether or not fear is behind your spouse's motivations, you must be patient with the active listening process in allowing the motivation to emerge. Active listening begins and ends with the promise of unconditional love for your spouse. Just as fear is a powerful motivator, so is love. And, as noted in 1 John 4:18, perfect love casts out all fear. As you allow this offering of love for your spouse to become the prominent motivator in your marriage, emotional intimacy will follow.

Insight Considers Intention

Understanding motivation matters, but it is incomplete. Insight also requires an acknowledgement of your partner's good intentions toward the relationship. Any time you engage your spouse verbally or nonverbally, you are communicating both content and relationship. The meaning of content is usually clear: If we are talking about who picks up which kids when, we're talking about picking up the kids. Every interaction in marriage also conveys relational value through nonverbal exchange, and this meaning, communicated intentionally or unintentionally, impacts the relationship dynamic.

Think of this intention toward the relationship in investment terms. You invest in your marriage when you intentionally build it up, or at least commit to doing no intentional harm to it. You withdraw from your marriage when your actions intentionally disrupt it. Therefore, as you think about offering insight, you must be able to discern those times when your respective intentions toward your marriage are an investment versus those times when they are a withdrawal. When your intention focuses on nurturing and encouraging the strengths of your spouse, you are doing everything in your power to demonstrate your commitment to relational investment. On the other hand, absent this nurturing and encouragement, it is quite likely that your spouse will perceive you as more invested in your own personal desires; this perception insidiously divests your marriage.

Let us expand on the investment analogy to clarify the role of intention. What happens when there is a hot stock on Wall Street? Investors are driving the value of the stock up, risking their own capital in hopes of a big return. As the value of this hot stock continues to climb, this breeds more investor confidence, leading to even more investment in the stock. But, what about the other side? When investors do not have confidence in the stock, they start to withdraw their capital in order to minimize their risk. The more investors bail out of the stock, the more the value of the stock plummets, obviously making it an unattractive investment option to most.

Spouses are like stock investors when it comes to intent in marriage. If my words and deeds make my wife feel that I am positively invested in her and the marriage, she will interpret most of my behaviors through this lens—driving the stock of our marriage relationship higher. But, absent this positive sentiment, any questionable behaviors will be interpreted negatively, divesting the relational value of the marriage. A therapist friend I know strives for her couples to attain an assumption of good will as the first lens through which they view interactions.

**Crafting your language and actions so that
your spouse directs positive attributions to you
is a central element of authentic marriage.**

Attribution Fuels Insight

This dynamic, known as *attribution* in psychology, holds tremendous power in marriage. Crafting your language and actions so that your spouse directs positive attributions to you is a central element of authentic marriage. Conversely, adjusting your own lens as a listener will make it less likely that you misattribute your partner's intent. Negative attributions inevitably cause a downward spiral in marriage. To what do you most commonly attribute the actions of your spouse?

Vicky's ability and interest in offering insight to Alan depends on whether she discerns that he really values her and their relationship. If she does not feel valued, she is likely to interpret Alan's behavior as yet another example of selfishness. However, if despite her disappointment, she feels valued by him, she will more likely attribute his behavior to other causes, thus preserving relational value in the marriage.

This has been my experience with Dalia. When I truly believe that Dalia's intention is to respect and defend me and our marriage, I more naturally interpret all of her behaviors through that investment lens. As I use this lens to see her strengths and her weaknesses, I gain true insight into her heart and mind, and our emotional intimacy is strengthened.

As you seek understanding of intention and motivation, the emotional intimacy in your marriage will reach heights never before achieved. Like so many paths to richer intimacy, the process is not always easy. It requires that both of you regulate your defensive reactions when hearing painful remarks from the other. But, Gideon's lesson teaches us to go with the strength that we have. Gideon's vignette models this willingness to express deep emotion. Gideon told God about his feeling of abandonment by his God, who had made promises to him. This was coupled with Gideon's feelings of inferiority. How often do feelings of abandonment and inferiority fester beneath the surface of your marriage?

Despite Gideon's negative sentiment, he felt safe expressing these negative deep emotions to God. In the same way, you need to be a safe harbor for your spouse's emotional expression. As the old adage goes, God gave each of us two ears and one mouth. This gives us divine insight into the proportion of listening to talking that God deems necessary to survival!

Insightful Tips

Your challenge is to reach beyond the surface-level emotions that you may more typically use and identify an emotion that better captures the intensity of your feelings, positive or negative. As you do, look for God to provide signs of divine presence just as the Lord did for Gideon. Try these tips to improve the emotional intimacy in your marriage when offered as first fruit:

1. Actively listen for insight into your spouse's motivation (desires and fears). When you believe that you have an insight, ask your spouse in a nonthreatening way if your assessment is correct.
2. Actively listen to appreciate your spouse's intent. If you discern negative intent, this is a sign that outside assistance from a trained professional may be necessary.
3. Tell your spouse about what motivates you.
4. Tell your spouse the value that he or she has to you.
5. Pursue insightful communication. If you find it difficult to communicate those deep emotions, begin with the less threatening emotions. But, try to communicate your emotions several times a week. Make an effort to become more comfortable expressing deeper emotions. Ideally, strive to communicate relationally every day. (NOTE: If you are in an unsafe relationship, this tip is unlikely to be healthy and should probably be avoided until an outside mediator can be engaged to assist in the process.)

WE HAVE BEEN discussing the effective use of touch and insight in building authentic marriage. On a scale of 1 to 5, where 1 is "Not a clue" and 5 is "Intimately familiar," how much insight do you think your spouse has into your motivations and intentions in the marriage right now? Write down some examples. How do you feel about this? What can you do to make it better?

Active listening is a key aspect of understanding motivation and intentionality. Write down those topics about which you and your spouse demonstrate: (1) good active listening and (2) poor active listening.

Offering Mutuality

The third TIME element is mutuality. *Mutuality* is a term and action used too infrequently in the marriage vocabulary. In its most basic sense, mutuality connotes benefit for both husband and wife. Offering mutuality suggests that both partners are concerned with promoting a balanced marriage in which each feels his or her needs and desires are equally validated. Emotional intimacy is an outgrowth of this validation.

If you are like most, you entered marriage believing that the person you married would prioritize your needs and desires. You believed that you were entering into a safe relationship. When you offer mutuality to your spouse you affirm these beliefs. In a culture full of selfishness, spouses offering mutuality are a gift from God.

There is no single best way to offer mutuality. It is offered in marital decisions as you allow your spouse's thinking to cultivate your own, or as you consider the positive or negative impact certain social relationships may have on your spouse. You offer mutuality when your nonverbal expressions of unconditional love for your spouse match your verbal declarations. But, be assured that Satan does not condone mutuality. His tactics to disrupt mutuality have not changed since the Garden of Eden, when self-centered pleasure-seeking was elevated above God-centered obedience. Let us examine how this distortion of God's intent introduced one of the most devastating forces into marriage: imbalanced power.

The Power Shift

In considering mutuality, it is important to think about God's original design of male and female. We earlier discussed that God describes the woman as man's counterpart. Although in Genesis 2 Adam was created first, God's plan for marriage entailed part and counterpart. There is no indication that God originally intended Eve's person, desires, or ideas to be less valuable than those of Adam. Before sin, Adam and Eve appear to be of equal power, different but jointly suitable. It is only after sin enters the world through the serpent's deception that God says in Genesis 3:16 (NRSV) "your desire shall be for your husband, and he shall rule over you." *Rule over you* is our first indication that sin has caused a power imbalance.

The natural question, then, is whether God ideally desires your marriage to look like the pre-fall egalitarian model or the post-fall hierarchical one. I believe that Scripture speaks clearly for the former. Ephesians offers these verses: "Be subject to one another out of reverence for Christ. Wives, be subject to your husbands as to the Lord. For the husband is the head of the wife just as Christ is the head of the church, the body of which he is the Savior. Just as the church is subject to Christ, so also wives ought to be, in everything, to their husbands" (Ephesians 5:21-24, NRSV). But, in order to surmise from these verses that husbands are divinely appointed power brokers in marriage, one must ignore verse 21 and the remainder of the chapter (Ephesians 5:25-33), which instruct the husband to demonstrate toward his wife the same love that Christ showed for the church. The message of the combined text is the undeniable responsibility of each spouse to be cast as servant to the other.

Throughout the New Testament, Jesus rejects the use of power to control others and affirms the use of power to serve. Rather than focusing on a unidirectional form of submissiveness from wife to husband, authors Jack and Judy Balswick propose that Ephesians 5 is a bidirectional alternative:

> Authority in Christian marriage involves dual submission to the lordship of Christ and to one another. . . . From this it is clear that headship, if that is the view one espouses, is to be understood not in the hierarchical sense of the husband's lording it over his wife, but rather in the sense of taking the role of a suffering servant. Christ's example as a compassionate servant who gave his life for his bride, the church, is the model of how the husband is to act as head. Wives too are called to this same self-giving, suffering-servant role. Mutual submissiveness then is the overriding message of Ephesians 5.[5]

Mutual submission or mutuality conveys a balance, particularly in relation to power. Western culture, especially within the Christian subculture, is built on patriarchy (imbalanced power). Generations of social systems and institutions have empowered the male at the female's expense. This imbalance of power, often emboldened by misinterpretations of Ephesians 5:21-24, can become abusive when husbands demand that their wives' beliefs, ideas, dreams, time, energy, priorities, and ministries are less important than their own.

Husbands, however, are not the only culprits. Wives often exert their power through verbal sparring in which they simply outlast their less vocal husbands. In some instances, wives use their influence over the children to gain the children's loyalty against their husbands. Yet, wives' most commonly abused use of power is in refusing to give themselves sexually to their husbands. I am reminded of a conference in which a wife blatantly admitted that withholding sex from her husband is the only power that she has in the relationship. While there are probably specific instances where this is a legitimate tactic, the long-term use of this strategy may be a catastrophic power play in your marriage.

The key point here is that both husbands and wives have sinned in abusing power. Imbalanced power is indeed contrary to the sharing theme emphasized by offering. True power in marriage is found when balance is negotiated. Negotiation is the godly response to a power imbalance. You might be tempted here to believe that the solution is simply permitting your spouse to get his or her way in a given disagreement. This is inaccurate, for the very act of permitting suggests that you are still using your power. The challenge is to transform power from being wielded by an individual to being embraced by a partnership.

Tips for Balancing Power in Your Marriage

In summary, offering mutuality requires both husbands and wives to make an ideological shift from imbalance to balance. We husbands must value our wives' input and perspectives as equal to our own. God did not create men as intellectually or creatively superior to women. So, the notion that husbands have a divine right to be the final arbiter of decisions in marriage lacks theological merit when examined in the full context of Scripture.

I fully recognize that this topic has long been debated in Christian circles. Exhaustive theological examination of this issue is certainly beyond the scope of this book—and is probably useless in improving the intimacy in your marriage. My hope, however, is that the following five mutuality tips will help you and your spouse negotiate a balanced relationship that improves the emotional intimacy in your marriage when offered as first fruit:

1. It can be difficult to see your own abuse of power. Pray for insight into this dynamic in your marriage. Then consider one thing that you can do to share power with your spouse.
2. Ask your spouse to tell you how you make him or her feel disempowered in the marriage. Accept the responses without defending yourself.
3. If your spouse is willing to listen, share those instances when you feel disempowered in the marriage and the deep emotions that this elicits. Avoid sounding accusatory.
4. When you and your spouse disagree on a decision to be made, search your own heart to discern whether you are making a power play.
5. Commit to serving your spouse each week with one offering that your spouse deems acceptable. The offering should be an act of service, not a gift. Remember that the acceptability of the offering is determined by your spouse, not by you.

Offering Encouragement

The final TIME element that spouses must offer is encouragement. Is your spouse a source of encouragement for you? The answer in many marriages is a resounding no. While the importance of encouragement is obvious, its absence in many marriages is obvious. When did you last encourage your spouse?

If you recall your premarriage days, your encouraging words and deeds to your spouse were likely overflowing. They probably convinced your spouse that you would forever be a source of encouragement. This, in fact, is what spouses should expect of each other. However, as marriage proceeds, encouragement tends to wane, because spouses become more centered on their own issues than their spouse's. Furthermore, the more conflict-laden your marriage is, the less you actually care about your spouse's feelings of discouragement. However, I believe that the most common reason that husbands and wives do not adequately encourage one another is an incorrect sense that our spouses do not actually need encouragement.

I believe that the most common reason that husbands and wives do not adequately encourage one another is an incorrect sense that our spouses do not actually need encouragement.

If you believe that your spouse is one of those people who doesn't need encouragement, research suggests that you are probably wrong. After interviewing seven hundred couples in eight U.S. cities, researchers found that both husbands and wives identified affirmation and encouragement as the fourth most important thing that they need from their spouses.[6] The disappointments and frustrations of everyday life wear on the minds of everyone. Yes, some people are better than others at encouraging themselves through the melee. But, as the survey results found, everyone benefits from a timely word of encouragement.

Ephesians 4:29 instructs us to "Let no evil talk come out of your mouths, but only what is useful for building up, as there is need, so that your words may give grace to those who hear"(NRSV). Encouragement builds emotional intimacy because it fosters empowerment. As your spouse internalizes your encouraging words, he or she feels more confident, even in the midst of difficult situations.

When offering encouragement, remember that it is important to phrase your intended words of encouragement in a manner that resonates with your spouse. If you try to encourage your spouse the way you like to be encouraged, it is unlikely to have the impact that you desire. Offering encouragement that is acceptable, just like all other offerings, requires that you do so in a manner that is acceptable to your spouse.

Keep in mind that it is not only the manner of the encouragement that is important but also the atmosphere in which it is offered. If you have a negatively charged marriage, your attempts at encouragement, if they are even offered, are likely to fall on deaf ears. Many people mistakenly believe that their words alone are sufficiently encouraging. This is usually not true. It is your empathetic presence that is encouraging. Your words are simply an expression of your empathy for your spouse and an extension of your confidence in him or her.

In short, encouragement flourishes when it possesses these three attributes: (1) It communicates safety; (2) it respects uniqueness; and (3) it emphasizes strengths. When your encouraging words communicate safety, they confirm for your spouse that you are in this relationship unconditionally. One spouse does not have to worry about abandonment by the other in a crisis of desperation and fear. In a real sense, you encourage your spouse to climb to all that God has for him or her because you act as a safety net. By communicating safety you also suggest that you will be able to listen and contain your spouse's concerns without becoming threatened yourself.

Encouraging words also respect the unique perspective of your spouse. Your words should remind your partner that he or she is "fearfully and wonderfully made," as noted in Psalm 139:14. Just as God gave each of us a fingerprint that is distinct from all others, God has also filled each of us with unique passions, desires, and visions. As a marriage partner, your duty is to encourage your spouse's pursuit of those dreams.

Finally, your words of encouragement should emphasize your spouse's strengths, including the use of these strengths to fulfill God's purposes in his or her life. Your spouse experiences daily challenges that erode self-confidence. But Philippians 4:13 says that we have the ability to do all things through Christ's strength; offering this encouragement to your partner will bolster his or her fortitude.

Prioritize Encouragement in Marriage

Use the following five encouragement tips to build emotional intimacy when offered as first fruit:

1. Remember that there is nothing wrong with feeling discouraged. Most of the heroes in the Bible had such times. Ultimately, they relied on God's deliverance, and so must you.
2. Communicate when you feel discouraged. It may feel like your spouse does not care but he or she simply may not be paying enough attention to realize how you are feeling.
3. Actively listen to your spouse talk, and read body language for discouragement.
4. Ask your spouse to give you a list of the ways in which he or she would like to be encouraged. Each week pick one thing from that list and do it.
5. Consider specific ways in which you can be more encouraging to your spouse.

As you share chronological time with your spouse, you build a healthy dependency on each other. It just does not feel right not to be together. The yearning for the other's presence you felt during the courtship days can be regained. But, marital offerings also promote the sharing of touch, insight, mutuality, and encouragement. As you make these offerings, you communicate the high value and priority that you have for your marriage. Most importantly, you communicate to God your desire for a marriage that honors the Lord.

Claiming the Offering Stone

Claiming the offering stone is to claim spiritual, emotional, and sexual intimacy. Your feelings about the current state of your marriage do not dictate whether you can lay claim to this intimacy. It is the state of your offering that does. As the Lord did with Gideon, God is letting you know that the Holy Spirit is with you as you embark on the commission to liberate your marriage from self-centeredness and to love your spouse as Christ loves the church.

This means that you make your best effort to offer intimate first fruit to God; your spouse is a beneficiary of this love offering.

When you struggle with the stumbling stones and frustrations of everyday marriage, remember that your offerings of intimacy are to God first, because you are being obedient to God's instruction. Don't get me wrong. It is not an easy task to sustain this level of unconditional love. Like Gideon, you may feel that God has failed you and your marriage. You may wonder where God was when your husband abused you, how God allowed your wife to cheat on you, or why God permitted your relationship to be marred by health challenges. Although God allowed Gideon to question, the Lord did not directly respond to Gideon's interrogation and accusations. As noted earlier, God may not respond to your doubts and questions either.

As God assured Gideon, you have enough strength for the task already. This strength may be intrinsic fortitude, resolve, or forbearance; it may be extrinsic financial, social, or political capital. Regardless of its form, you and your spouse have within your reach all you need to carry out your commission for mutual intimacy.

Doubting God's Commission for Your Marriage

It is natural to question the commission of God. Gideon certainly did. Through Gideon's questions, however, we get a glimpse into his underlying self-doubt. Many of the difficulties in your marriage reflect your own insecurities. How might your fears and lack of self-confidence be impeding your path to the intimacy that you desire? Gideon put his feelings out there. He told God that he and his family were weak. I suspect that Gideon expected God to say something like, "Okay, Gideon. You're right. My mistake. You aren't the right person for the job."

What Gideon did not understand is something that we too struggle with. God uses the foolish things of the world to confound the wise, the weak things of the world to confound the strong (1 Corinthians 1:27). God's warfare is counterintuitive. Your weakness is integral to the commission. You may feel that everyone else's marriage is better than yours or that there is nothing special about yours. God wants your confession to highlight how insufficient to the task you are, because it is in this weakness that God shows off. Victory is in God's strength and your weakness, when that weakness is offered to God.

It can be difficult to believe in a victorious outcome when you are mired in negative circumstances, when every fiber in your body is screaming, "Get out!" We ask God, "Are you sure about this?" We, like Gideon, want a sign that God is really in this. Gideon obtained the confirmation that he desired only after he was obedient to the Lord's directions for an acceptable offering.

The lessons of Gideon witness that God is an active presence in your marriage. In the midst of your Scripture reading, praying, fasting, and bowing your knees before the Lord, you question whether the Lord is with your marriage. Your doubts about whether you married the right person and whether you love your spouse anymore prompt you to doubt God's willingness to do the miraculous. But, Gideon reminds us that God is asking for our obedience even within the context of a strained marital relationship. And, since the fall of humanity, obedience to God has always necessitated sacrificial offerings. Your marriage is no exception.

Much of your marital travail exists because God has not accepted the offerings that you have brought before him. God may have rejected your prayers for marital healing, authentic love, sexual fulfillment, and covenant partnership because you and your spouse have not honored or been obedient to the Lord's rules of engagement. The military goes to great measures to train its soldiers on combat protocol. The terms of its warfare are documented so that everyone can operate seamlessly, even under periods of duress and life-threatening situations.

God has also given us our rules of engagement as we battle the physical, emotional, and spiritual forces that seek to kill, steal, and destroy our marriages. The most important rule of engagement is to have the Lord by your side. This is the essence of our faith journey. The Bible consistently identifies us as living sacrifices. Given that God accepts unblemished sacrifices only, you must present yourself as a holy and acceptable offering (Romans 12:1). This rule of engagement extends to your marriage.

I ROCK Exercises

Scripture Memorization: Ephesians 5:1-2, NRSV

Therefore be imitators of God, as beloved children, and live in love, as Christ loved us and gave himself up for us, a fragrant offering and sacrifice to God.

Contemplation

Respond to the following points of contemplation in your personal journal:

1. Think about the touch, insight, mutuality, and encouragement that exist in your marriage. How acceptable have your offerings in each of these areas been to your spouse? How satisfied are you with your spouse's offerings? Your marriage will be enriched by your mutual commitment to the tips that are enumerated in each area.

2. According to 1 Corinthians 1:27, God uses the foolish things of the world to confound the wise, the weak things to confound the strong. Summarize the individual weaknesses that you are willing to offer to God.

3. How might your weaknesses empower you to minister to others?

Integration

4. Which of the TIME elements is most meaningful to you? Which one has the least meaning to you? How aware is your spouse of this? In which area do you need more from your spouse? Take some time to respond in your journal.

We ROCK Exercises

Contemplation

1. Remembering that *offering* means "to draw close," discuss together how to adjust the rules of engagement in your marriage to grow closer to God and to each other.

Integration

2. As a couple, identify real-life, practical things that you would do over the next three to six months, if you were having the same struggles as Alan and Vicky, our couple in this chapter. Use the time, insight, mutuality, and encouragement tips to guide your plan.

   a. What do you think may be their biggest challenges to turning things around?

   b. What, if any, aspects of their marriage are similar to qualities of your own marriage?

3. As a couple, sit facing each other. Express to each other the one aspect of TIME that you need from your spouse by filling in the blanks in the following sentence: I need more _____ from you, because without it I feel _____.

PART FOUR

Discovering Covenant
The Rock of Boundaries

Love does not consist in gazing at each other
but in looking together in the same direction.
—Antoine de Saint-Exupéry

By now it is certainly evident to you that a healthy marriage requires a commitment to work. As you work towards being mutually redemptive and strengthening your intimacy profile, your partnership is an offering that bellows a sweet-smelling savor to God. However, in your efforts to unify and meet your spouse's needs, it is important to maintain a clear sense of your identity. Being the best you is actually necessary to having your best marriage. This brings us to the third rock in the ROCKS model, Covenant. This rock teaches us the importance of personal and marital boundaries.

"Come now, let us make a covenant, you and I; and let it be a witness between you and me." So Jacob took a stone, and set it up as a pillar. And Jacob said to his kinfolk, "Gather stones," and they took stones, and made a heap; and they ate there by the heap. Laban called it Jegar-sahadutha [the heap of witness]: but Jacob called it Galeed. Laban said, "This heap is a witness between you and me today." Therefore he called it Galeed, and the pillar Mizpah [the watchpost], for he said, "The LORD watch between you and me, when we are absent one from the other. If you ill-treat my daughters, or if you take wives in addition to my daughters, though no one else is with us, remember that God is witness between you and me."

Then Laban said to Jacob, "See this heap and see the pillar, which I have set between you and me. This heap is a witness, and the pillar is a witness, that I will not pass beyond this heap to you, and you will not pass beyond this heap and this pillar to me, for harm. May the God of Abraham and the God of Nahor,"—the God of their father—"judge between us." So Jacob swore by the Fear of his father Isaac (Genesis 31:44-53, NRSV).

CHAPTER 9

Step 6: Check the Boundaries of Your Marriage

You cover the LORD's altar with tears, with weeping and
groaning because he no longer regards the offering or accepts
it with favor at your hand. You ask, "Why does he not?"
Because the LORD was a witness between you and
the wife of your youth, to whom you have been faithless,
though she is your companion and your wife by covenant.
–Malachi 2:13-14, NRSV

Covenant: A Binding Agreement

The flexibility of African American family structure has a rich history and storied tradition; the term *family* is not simply a matter of bloodlines. The African American family has adapted to social and economic injustices by contracting and expanding as necessary to survive as a community. It is normal even now for there to be little distinction between siblings and cousins or between uncles and dear family friends. How many people do you call *uncle, aunt,* or *cousin* to whom you have no actual blood ties? It is common to find African American families who have formally and informally fostered and adopted children. Sisters have taken legal responsibility for the children of incarcerated or otherwise incapacitated siblings, and wayward teens have gone to live with uncles and aunts to help the teens get their lives together.

Perhaps more than any other American subculture, the African American family represents a complex network of relationships that sociologists have dubbed a *kinship network* to account for the interrelatedness of meaningful formal and informal relationships. These kinship networks are effectively social welfare systems, allowing resources to be shared as needs arise. The boundaries between yours and ours, blood and non-blood are blurred. While these kinship networks are clearly an African American community strength, they often pose challenges for African American marriages.

Authentic marriages must be able to respond to kinship needs when desired but must be able to draw clear lines around the husband–wife relationship. This is even more complicated in situations in which economic needs force couples to live with or otherwise depend on a parent, grandparent, or others in the kinship system. Therefore, it is important to understand and establish effective boundaries in the marriage. African American couples who understand God's intent for covenant will then possess the tools necessary to establish and maintain these boundaries, without dishonoring the kinship network. The story of Jacob and Laban is the backdrop for this important lesson.

Jacob's Lessons in Boundary Setting

Throughout this book, I have asserted that discovering authentic marriage is ultimately a shift from *I* to *we*, from selfishness to selflessness—without losing one's individuality. We now examine the life of another of the Old Testament patriarchs, Jacob, as we grapple with understanding marriage as covenant. Burdened with self-centeredness and deceit, Jacob was transformed through wrestling with God into a man worthy of being renamed Israel ("exalted father") by God. Jacob's journey is one of sanctification through suffering, and it occurred in stages. His experience with his uncle Laban, as excerpted above, is one of the turning points. For thirteen years, Jacob and Laban had deceived and lied to each other in order to gain advantage in their relationship as father-and son-in-law. Jacob's transformation may be better understood if we begin by recapping how Jacob came to be in the company of his uncle.

Even before Jacob's birth, God decreed an astonishing inheritance upon Jacob (Genesis 25:23). Jacob, however, was inclined to manipulate circumstances for his own ends, rather than relying on God to keep his promise. Amazingly, Jacob's aggression began while he was still in the womb, as he and his twin brother, Esau, were jostling with each other so much that their mother, Rebecca, asked the LORD about it. At birth, Jacob exited his mother's womb with his hand grasping the heel of Esau, who was born first. Talk about encroaching on another's space!

As Jacob grew, he continued to assert himself by any means necessary to get what he desired. You might say that his tendency toward deceit was transgenerational, passing to Jacob from his mother, Rebecca.

Scripture tells us that Rebecca loved Jacob more than his brother, Esau, even as Isaac favored his older son. This love translated into an unhealthy alignment between Rebecca and Jacob, and was a central dynamic in their plot to steal the blessing and birthright from Jacob's father, Isaac, and his brother, Esau, respectively. Although Jacob successfully executed this treachery, he angered his brother to the point that he received a death threat, a threat that forced him to flee his homeland. Jacob and his mother arranged a journey to the home of her brother Laban, whom Jacob would soon learn was as deceptive as he.

Jacob labored for Laban for seven years in order to win Laban's daughter Rachel in marriage. We first witness Laban's cunning when he secretly switches his elder daughter, Leah, for Rachel. This began a cycle of deceit that continued for thirteen years.

But, as we pick up the vignette of Jacob in Genesis 31, we see another step in Jacob's maturity. He begins to make his own choices, rather than continuing to be manipulated by the choices of others. Not surprisingly, Laban is upset by Jacob's newfound sense of ownership. As often happens in families when a young person matures, Laban pursued Jacob to bring him back to what had been the "normal" way of doing things. But, Jacob had made a decision to leave an ungodly system in favor of a more excellent way, so Laban's efforts were fruitless.

Jacob determined to take his portion of earnings and to leave the land of his uncle as well as the inherent conflict. Laban and Jacob's covenant, symbolized by piles of rock, is the agreement that they will never invade one another's territory with the purpose of doing harm. This boundary of rocks was pronounced for their servants to witness. In essence, the boundary was negotiated to resolve conflict before it can start. The very location was called *Mizpah*, which meant "the watchtower," to signify that God would be watching their adherence to the covenant. Mizpah becomes a key moment for Jacob. He begins to relate to God in a new way by making amends for the deceit and boundary violations that he had caused previously. Later, Jacob returns to his homeland to seek forgiveness from his brother, Esau.

Finding We in Me

The rocks at Mizpah are a concrete representation of a binding agreement. Unfortunately, the covenant boundaries in our marriages are not always so clearly defined. Much of the emotional tumult in marriage is a result of poor boundaries. It is difficult to establish healthy boundaries because so few of us come from families in which this concept was modeled and lived out. For many of us, the kinship network, rather than the conventional two-parent model, taught us the lessons of life. In many cases, however, healthy boundaries were a casualty of this system. Our community often requires siblings to serve as parents for younger siblings. We need grandparents to serve parental functions, because of the immaturity or inaccessibility of capable parents. Furthermore, individual needs are often neglected as the family's scarce physical and emotional resources are stretched too thin. Although the African American community has shown amazing resilience, many of us do not know what individual or marital boundaries look like, much less how to protect them. We have a lot in common with Jacob. Just as Jacob was the product of dysfunctional family boundaries, so are many of us.

Creating healthy boundaries is central to preventing and resolving marital conflict and living a covenant marriage. In the next section, we will take a closer look at exactly what healthy boundaries look like. How healthy are the interactions in your family? Are you a product of relationships that are rigid or enmeshed? If so, you are probably exhibiting some of those same tendencies in your marriage. What personal and marital boundaries need adjusting in your life? These are all questions for you to think about as you read through this chapter.

Boundaries are easily muddied in marital relationships because American culture touts the virtue of a couple becoming one once the marriage bands are exchanged; in fact, our wedding ceremonies incorporate specific rituals to diminish our individuality (I-ness) and elevate unity (We-ness). This does not seem like a bad thing on the surface, but when engaged in uncritically, it can foster a loss of self-identity. Unfortunately, many well-intended secular and Christian marriages have contributed to this distortion of the meaning of unity.

> **LABAN AND JACOB** named the location of their covenant *Mizpah* to signify that God watches—holding them responsible to do no harm to each other. God watches your marital interactions with this same attentiveness. Have you crossed the line and done harm to your spouse's identity or confidence in whom the person God created him or her to be? Are there ways in which you keep your spouse from pursuing God's purpose for his or her life? Keep in mind that sometimes inaction is the worst violation of all (as you will see in the story of Kelvin and Brianna).

I think back to my own wedding ceremony years ago, when Dalia and I lit our unity candle. Like many other couples, we followed this symbolic act by blowing out the candles that represented our individual selves. At the time I appreciated this ritual, but today I question it. What does it mean to "blow out" my own individuality? Can we become one yet retain our individuality? While discovering authentic meaning in marriage necessitates a shift from a self-centered to a we-centered paradigm, you can only understand we-centeredness by understanding yourself. In other words, discovering marital unity requires discovery of yourself, which requires boundaries delineating where you end and where your partner begins. The tension between *I* and *we* in marriage and family relationships is a constant source of growth and challenge in self-discovery and self-awareness. This journey is difficult because it is a fluid process, as your feelings, attitudes, beliefs, values, and aspirations shift over time.

The tension between *I* and *we* in marriage and family relationships is a constant source of growth and challenge in self-discovery and self-awareness.

Understanding the Boundaries of Your Marriage

In recent years, particularly with the advent of what some call *hyperindividualism*, discussions and books on personal boundaries among Christians and non-Christians are plentiful. For example, Cloud and Townsend's popular book, *Boundaries*, revolutionized thinking among Christian and secular audiences about the importance of rejecting chaotic or rigid boundaries and gravitating toward permeable boundaries, which are strong yet flexible.[1]

Unhealthy Boundaries

Unhealthy boundaries are the result of sin. Before the entry of sin into the world, the relationships among humans, and between humans and God, were characterized by harmony. Sin, however, fractured this harmony, causing separation on many levels. Ever since, we humans have been searching for means to reconnect. This inner desire for reconnection drives us to seek care from our partners in ways that are often more destructive than connecting. To further examine these boundary issues, I would like to introduce you to Kelvin and Brianna.

Kelvin and Brianna, a young couple married for only two years, are currently living separately due to the marital problems they are experiencing. Within the past month, Kelvin has moved out of the apartment where he and Brianna lived with Brianna's mother and grandmother. They have been in this living arrangement since they married, in order to become financially stable. Although he is working toward a business degree at a community college at night while continuously searching for a permanent job, Kelvin has had difficulty getting more than temporary employment. Brianna, who received her bachelor's degree in accounting, has steady employment, but a large portion of her check supports her mother and grandmother, with the remainder paying off school and car loans. So, Kelvin and Brianna have been unable to save money to get their own place.

Kelvin, who was raised by his mother and older brother, has moved back to his mother's apartment after a heated argument with Brianna's mother. Kelvin was furious that Brianna remained silent when her mother accused him of being a lazy, deadbeat husband who was not good enough for her daughter. After retaliating with a few curse words, Kelvin grabbed some clothes, gave Brianna a cold stare, and left the apartment. Two days later, Kelvin and Brianna have yet to talk.

In our marriages, we are likely to engage in the behaviors that worked for us in our own families. For example, if you came from a family that yelled a lot, you are likely to yell at your partner as a way of attempting to get him or her to meet your needs. If you came from a family who withdrew and pouted following arguments, you are also likely to withdraw in the hope that someone follows you to care for you. Kelvin's hasty withdrawal from this conflict is a prime example. Is he assuming that Brianna will come chasing? After two days, it should be obvious that she won't. Of course, the fact that Brianna remained silent during the conflict and allowed Kelvin to go without saying a word to him speaks volumes as well. This couple is in trouble. The longer they go without talking, the more damage the marriage experiences. Both have erred in judgment. These errors are mostly boundary issues that probably have been fueled by their respective families of origin.

Unless they understand the boundary issues, they will continue in this cycle—if their fragile marriage survives the current crisis.

How did Kelvin and Brianna develop these patterns? These are, in fact, common behaviors that are used to protect self-identify, to keep us from feeling wounded, and to soothe our fears in our early lives. As adults, we may continue to rely on them to deal with discomfort or pain in our marriages, despite the fact that they were dysfunctional then and are dysfunctional now.

Rigid Boundaries

As children some of us were required to heed overly controlling parents, without regard for our own feelings or concerns. In some families, feelings of love and belonging were affirmed only to the degree that you abandoned your own desires and went along with what your parents wanted. Many of these families were and are dangerously controlling and isolating in their views of those outside of the family. In essence, you were rewarded for thinking, feeling, and aspiring toward what was defined as "right" by this family. If you were raised in such a family, your experience reinforces the idea that rejection of family wishes will result in your abandonment by your family. And, in the most heinous family systems, failure to go along with the family desires can manifest as physical, sexual, and emotional abuse.

Loose Boundaries

In other families, parents were unavailable (due to demanding jobs or substance abuse, for example) or unwilling to demonstrate appropriate limits for children. Adults who are products of these families tend to have their identities and emotions dependent upon the approval of others. This is normal to some extent in all families; however, if your family of origin depended on these behaviors to more severe degrees, you are likely to have unhealthy boundaries in your marriage, whether loose or rigid.

When your boundaries are loose, it leads to enmeshed relationships, the kind of relationships in which the individuals appear to be unable to function without the other. There is often a complementarity to this enmeshment. For example, there are a few devastatingly homesick college students whose mothers can't seem to cut the apron strings and call every day to make sure they drank their milk at breakfast. Enmeshed relationships are unhealthy because they are characterized by inability to or difficulty in distinguishing your desires and wishes apart from someone else's. People who gravitate toward enmeshed relationships cannot set firm personal boundaries, because they fear they will be unloved if they do not let the other in on demand—or that the other will punish them if they try.

Brianna, in my opinion, has serious enmeshment issues with her mother and grandmother. In allowing her mother to separate her from her husband, she has effectively given her mother unhealthy authority in her marriage. Brianna has allowed her mother to be her voice, tacitly approving her mother's comments. Kelvin, though, is not without fault. His willingness to run to his own mother in the heat of conflict shows the poor boundaries that he has with his mom.

In other situations, rigid boundaries lead to disconnected relationships in which independence is touted as something of a holy grail. This is the family where parents send their children off to college with the expectation that they may not even speak to one another until Christmas, and that's fine with everyone. It's been years since they shared dinner time with one another anyway—a family with practically no connection to one another at all.

> **Any kind of unhealthy boundary makes covenant marriage difficult, because such boundaries are contradictory to the concept of mutuality.**

Any kind of unhealthy boundary makes covenant marriage difficult, because such boundaries are contradictory to the concept of mutuality. If you worry about whether your spouse will love you if you show disappointment in him or her, or if you become angry with your spouse for having views different from your own, then boundary issues may be a problem.

God is watching the boundaries you set. He assesses the extent to which your boundaries are too flexible or too rigid. Like Jacob and Laban, you and your spouse should respect these drawn boundaries, not crossing them to do spiritual, emotional, or physical harm to one another. God nudges you through Scripture and through your relationships with others to maintain permeable or flexible boundaries, which you can adjust as necessary. Failure to heed this nudge inevitably results in God using more drastic measures to communicate the severity of the issue.

Healthy boundaries are needed so that you can see yourself in relation to God who, the Scriptures tell us, watches you. The Lord sees us when we are feeling negative or spiteful, but God also watches moments of redemption and offering. Understanding boundaries gives meaning and context to your sacrifice, which is why Mizpah is such a pivotal transition point in your marriage. Kelvin and Brianna need to find their Mizpah—and so do you and your spouse. There, Kelvin and Brianna, and you and your spouse can accept and submit to God the baggage that has limited you from fully investing in your marriage, from fully believing in each other, and from fully trusting God's decree of victory in your marriage.

I ROCK Exercises

Scripture Memorization: Matthew 20:26-28, NRSV

Whoever wishes to be great among you must be your servant, and whoever wishes to be first among you must be your slave; just as the Son of Man came not to be served but to serve, and to give his life a ransom for many.

Contemplation

Respond to the following points of contemplation in your personal journal:

1. What aspects of your individuality have been diminished or lost within your marriage? Has this made your marriage better or worse?
2. What aspects of your marriage feel we-centered to you? What aspects feel me-centered? How do you feel about the me-centeredness in parts of your marriage?

3. Think about the type of boundaries that existed in the family in which you grew up. Which type of boundary (rigid, enmeshed, permeable) best describes your relationship with your parents or how you saw your parents relate to each other? It may be different for each parent. In what ways are your relational boundaries with your spouse similar and dissimilar from those you had with your parents?

Integration

1. Take another unmarked copy of your family history profile that you created in Chapter 2 and proceed through the following five steps:

   Step 1: Write on these sheets "My Family Boundaries."

   Step 2: Place a circle around each couple that you think has an overly controlling, demanding, or rigid (including domestic violence) relationship.

   Step 3: Place a triangle around each couple that you think has personal boundaries that are too loose (one individual seems to nearly always prioritize the preferences, opinions, and desires of his or her spouse over his or her own in a manner that minimizes his or her own uniqueness).

   Step 4: Place a square around each couple that you perceive has healthy personal boundaries (where both partners appear to value and support the preferences, opinions, and desires of each other).

   Step 5: How do the boundaries in your marriage compare to others in your extended family?

We ROCK Exercises

Contemplation

1. *Mizpah* means "the watchtower," suggesting that God is watching over the covenant. As a couple, discuss what boundary issues exist in your marriage that you are ashamed for God to see.

2. Without covenant boundaries in your marriage, your relationship will always have elements of distrust. What commitments

are you able to make to your spouse in securing healthier, God-centered boundaries for yourself?

Integration

1. Compare the family history profiles you each developed in this unit's I ROCK exercise. In what ways are your respective "My Family Boundaries" histories similar and different?
2. Discuss the ways in which the history of boundaries in your respective families contributes to the level of trust in your marriage right now.

CHAPTER 10

Step 7: Keep Covenant
in Your Conflict

*All married couples should learn the art of battle
as they should learn the art of making love.
Good battle is objective and honest—never vicious
or cruel. Good battle is healthy and constructive, and
brings to a marriage the principle of equal partnership.*
—ANN LANDERS

Fighting for Healthy Boundaries

Boundaries give covenant meaning as they offer proper limitations. Boundaries limit the activities in which I engage. Boundaries protect my marriage from forces that seek to destroy it. Boundaries give me confidence and trust in the special relationship that Dalia and I share. In other words, boundaries are critical to the ROCKS model because they establish the content for covenant. Yet boundaries also have the potential to cause conflict. Our goal in this chapter is to understand how to preserve healthy boundaries even when conflict happens—because, as you know, conflict inevitably comes.

As Christians, we value covenant because Scripture tells us that it reflects the nature of our relationship with God. God's covenant with the Hebrew people in the Old Testament was built upon thousands of rules and ordinances governing the lives of the people. Since humans could not observe these rules perfectly, God instituted a system of repentance and offering to restore covenant. This same system exists in marriage—repentance and offering enable the restoration of healthy boundaries. Ultimately, God provided Jesus to suffer that we might live, and as such, his sacrifice is the new covenant that provides us access to God's throne.

However, even as God requires us to be in covenant, the Lord requires us to be flexible in adapting to myriad situations, without losing our sense of self or our love for our God. With this lens, we examine Christ's comparison of his relationship with the church as the inspiration for our marriages. Just as Christ's life and death gave the Old Testament laws new meaning, Christ instructs that our marriages bring new meaning into a culture that glorifies rules and systems that are counter to God's kingdom culture.

With this in mind, I suggest that covenant is a binding agreement characterized by healthy boundaries. The rocks at Mizpah illustrate the importance of clearly agreed-upon boundaries. This is critical to our discussion, because many marriages have "agreed" to unhealthy rather than healthy boundaries, through the continual living of unwritten, unconsciously established, codependent rules.

Poor boundaries in the African American community, as in other ethnic communities, are often the result of compromising social and economic situations. Social stressors, such as the disproportionate number of incarcerated African American males, the number of single women with children, and the increasing education gap between African American males and females, weaken personal boundaries when males and females compromise their own identities or values in an effort to hold on to the relationship they have at any cost.

For example, if women perceive that available partners are scarce, some may falsely believe that it is better to have an abusive husband than to have no husband at all. Economic stressors, such as living with relatives or high unemployment in urban centers, can also destabilize boundaries, as couples fight over money and space issues. Because so many African Americans are raised with these socioeconomic inequities, we often lack the understanding and skills to develop healthier boundaries. The consequences are dire, as these couples struggle to know who they really are in the midst of chaos and conflict.

Remembering Mizpah

Let me ask an odd question: How agreeable is your marriage? *Agreeable* does not mean that you do not have conflicts. Ironically, the absence of conflict may indicate the presence of unhealthy boundaries. Agreement means that you make a conscious, daily commitment to pursue a binding relationship characterized by health. This requires that you remember Mizpah in everyday transactions—a place of respect for each other's spiritual, physical, and emotional boundaries. In this manner, your intention to do no harm to your marriage is best reflected.

Kelvin and Brianna's unhealthy boundaries are clearly doing harm to them as individuals and to their union. They have lost sight of Mizpah as they have allowed a myriad of very real social and economic factors to disrupt their marriage. Spiritually and physically, they have allowed subconscious forces and ungodly logic to push them apart. Issues of pride, stubbornness, and frustration have escalated the conflict by preventing them from seeing the disrespect they are showing to God and each other. Kelvin and Brianna do not seem to appreciate the idea that God is watching them, just as he watches all of our marriages.

Let's be realistic, though. It is difficult for us to see our own Mizpah violations. We may need others to help us—especially those who have a vested interest in helping us to build love, trust, and respect in our marriages. This is when trusted family and friends, marriage mentors, or professional therapists can be of great service.

MANY COUPLES live through conflict as if they are on a remote island without access to any help. Our minds play tricks on us, making us believe that we have too much to lose if we seek help or that others will not be able to understand. God, however, does not leave you in isolation. There are others who can help you if you reach out. Ask God to stretch your thinking. Who do you know that could objectively see the contours of your marriage and support its growth? Once you sense someone in your spirit, call that person immediately and let the Holy Spirit guide what you share.

It is difficult when our efforts to define and maintain healthy boundaries seem to create more conflict. This is frustrating, but frustratingly common. Your efforts may initially garner resistance from your spouse, because you are challenging what has become "normal." It is important that you expect and recognize this discomfort. Areas of disagreement challenge our personal and marital boundaries. Complaints and criticisms often evolve into feelings of contempt, as we become continually agitated by the conflicting perspectives of our spouses. As trust and respect wane, what began as tolerable and infrequent disagreements on important issues devolve into intolerable and constant disagreements about everything.

If this describes your relationship, I want to encourage you to hold on. Do not allow these conflicts to separate you as Kelvin and Brianna have done. In fact, these frustrations hold tremendous potential for developing authentic covenantal bonds. Believe it or not, conflict is actually the key to becoming closer to God in marriage. Disagreement promotes a spiritually, emotionally, and sexually fulfilling relationship, because it offers the opportunity for each partner to stretch beyond his or her comfort level with someone who is obviously different and challenging. Will disagreement and conflict represent a standing stone or a stumbling block? The answer depends on your joint ability to manage conflict constructively rather than being overcome by it.

Managing Conflict

Couples have conflict. In the early days of marriage, couples can minimize the destructive impact of the conflict. But in time, for better or worse, your individual reactions may default to the negative styles of your families of origin.

As these underlying factors become more prominent, it will become more difficult to resolve even minor issues without erupting in anger or disconnecting from each other. You are not alone: Research shows that 69 percent of married couples have conflict that is considered unresolvable.[1] Much of this unresolvable conflict is because spouses assume somewhat intractable positions that derive from the defenses of their basic personalities. Managing conflict, then, requires you both to understand your natural tendencies and defenses.

Remember, your ability to sustain covenant in your marriage is not a function of your ability to avoid conflict. Even wonderful marriages have conflict. It is a mistake to consider Kelvin and Brianna's current conflict as the only problem. While there are several boundary and communication issues that are fueling it, the separation and silence they are living with are manifestations of a much bigger problem. Again: The conflict is not the problem. This point must be emphasized, because couples often use such individual fights as indicators that they should not be married. This logic is fundamentally flawed. What couples must do is commit themselves to not harming the relationship when they experience conflict, actively listening to one another's concerns and discerning what is truly underneath the conflict. What really matters is your collective skill at conflict resolution—this is how healthy marriages remain wonderful.

At their core, conflict resolution skills in marriage are best understood as the faithful practice of redemption and offering. Whether your respective personalities lean toward more conflict-laden or conflict-avoidant interaction, redemption and offering communicate authentic forgiveness and emotional attachment that preserve the integrity of the relationship over the conflict at hand. Your ability to maintain covenantal boundaries in which you respect each other's perspective and feelings is the key to marital success.

The journey to covenant begins with understanding yourself as a separate and whole person apart from your spouse.

Here is an irony. The journey to covenant begins with understanding yourself as a separate and whole person apart from your spouse. In Kelvin's case, he needs to remember the unique gifts that God has given him as an individual. He should feel affirmed in his identity as an African American man who is doing his best to educate himself, to make a living in difficult circumstances, and to commit himself to one woman. These goals are laudable, and unfortunately they do not apply to enough men in the African American community.

Brianna must also see her individual gifts. She should feel confident in her education and her ability to sustain employment and predictable income. She should be applauded for remaining committed to her mother and grandmother who reared her. She has avoided many of the traps such as teenage pregnancy, academic complacency, and an entitlement attitude that snare too many young African American females.

Both Kelvin and Brianna need to embrace their individual strengths in order to make this marriage work without the improper influence of others. The Bible values individuality, highlighting the need to know and love ourselves. You are fearfully and wonderfully made, and while we are all designed in God's image, our Creator used a blueprint for you that is original.

Yet, we lose sight of our uniqueness and value, at times becoming so enmeshed with our spouses, children, friends, jobs, and churches that our individual value is lost even to us. We neglect to set healthy boundaries, because we fear that we will be less loved, less valued, and maybe even less godly if we do. For example, some of Brianna's poor boundaries may come from fear of her mother's rejection.

Covenant Marriage

The divine plan for your marriage is not that you lose yourself but rather that you find God. Marriage refines you and your relationship with the Lord by presenting peaks of ever increasing emotional complexity for you to climb. Therefore, in resolving your marital conflict, you are finding God. To me, this is the essence of covenant marriage.

Covenant marriage requires you to set boundaries around yourself, first as an individual distinct from your partner, and secondly as a couple distinct from the world. Jacob and Laban erected visible stones as a covenant to God and each other that neither would cross the boundary to do harm to the other. In fact, the vignette shows that the covenant really extended beyond these two men. Jacob vowed to Laban that he would not cross a boundary to do harm to his wives (Laban's daughters), either physically or by having relations with other women. In essence, Jacob's agreement was that he would do no harm to his marriages. Jacob and Laban's covenant at Mizpah illustrates five important truths about covenant-based marriage:

- Covenant marriage requires each spouse to know himself or herself.
- Covenant marriage values both individual and relational boundaries.
- Covenant marriage is a vow to protect and do no harm to your spouse.
- Covenant marriage uses managed conflict to mature us spiritually.
- Covenant marriage remembers that God, our Watchtower, observes our adherence to our vows.

God calls our marriages to be covenants that reflect his glory as two sinful humans sacrifice themselves to become a force that exceeds the sum of their parts as individuals. That is the synergy of marriage. Synergy, however, rarely comes without friction, certainly not in marriage. But this friction is what enhances the meaning in the covenant. As you deal with the differences in opinion and needs between you and your spouse you will continually bump up against each other's boundaries. This is normal. The key principle is to not allow the conflict to weaken your commitment to covenant. The Ann Landers quote at the beginning of this chapter provides a fitting conclusion as well. The friction inherent in good battles enhances your marriage by mutually stretching you toward equal partnership. It reminds me of the yoga classes that I have done that certainly create pain during the stretching exercise. But, these stretches lead to a healthier, better functioning me. And, so it will be for your marriage.

I ROCK Exercises

Scripture Memorization: 2 Corinthians 12:8-10, NRSV

Three times I appealed to the Lord about this, that it would leave me, but he said to me, "My grace is sufficient for you, for power is made perfect in weakness." So, I will boast all the more gladly of my weaknesses, so that the power of Christ may dwell in me. Therefore I am content with weaknesses, insults, hardships, persecutions, and calamities for the sake of Christ; for whenever I am weak, then I am strong.

Contemplation

Respond to the following points of contemplation in your personal journal:

1. What social, economic, or other stressors are creating boundary problems in your marriage?
2. Around what issues in your marriage is conflict most problematic? What spiritual issues might be behind this conflict?

Integration

3. In this section we have discussed Jacob's relational conflict. Find another instance in the Bible where there is protracted conflict between two people. What are the similarities and differences between these relational conflicts and the ones that you have? How similar or different are the spiritual issues underneath the conflict than yours?

We ROCK Exercises

Contemplation

1. Discuss your conflict resolution styles as individuals and as a couple. How have your respective styles of resolving conflict helped and harmed your marriage?
2. As a couple, discuss the boundary problems in your relationship that you realize have not been dealt with aggressively enough. How, if at all, have these issues affected your ability to have a covenant marriage?

Integration

3. Compare your answers from the I ROCK exercise #1. Make a single list, combining the stressors you each identified. Order this list from the most to the least stressful. Pick one of the stressors that you can do something about. Talk about a strategy to accomplish this goal. Proactively work to resolve this stressor over the next several weeks.

4. Review the five tenets of covenant marriage at the end of this chapter. Develop your own marital covenant, detailing what you each commit to do in order to satisfy these five objectives of covenant marriage. In other words, what will each of you practically commit to do to understand yourself more, to respect your own and each other's personal and relational boundaries, to protect one another, to manage your conflict, and to honor your vows? Once you have agreed to your marriage covenant, each of you should sign your name, pray over the covenant, and dedicate it to God as an offering.

PART FIVE

Knowledge:
The Rock of Power

My wife has been my closest friend, my closest advisor.
And . . . she's not somebody who looks to the limelight, or even
is wild about me being in politics. And that's a good reality check
on me. When I go home, she wants me to be a good father and
a good husband. And everything else is secondary to that.
—BARACK OBAMA

Since you began this journey through *Marriage ROCKS* the focus
has been centered on you and your spouse—integrating God's
will into your union. As you will soon see, the fourth rock takes
you from an internal examination of your marriage to an external assessment of your marriage's influence. To be clear, this rock
dubbed Knowledge is still about enriching your marriage. However, this enrichment will occur as you build upon those lessons
of redemption, offering, and covenant by modeling them to others with whom you come in contact. In this manner, your marriage will demonstrate the power that God has placed within
your union.

BIBLICAL VIGNETTE:
Joshua's Power Rock

When the entire nation had finished crossing over the Jordan, the LORD said to Joshua: "Select twelve men from the people, one from each tribe, and command them, 'Take twelve stones from here out of the middle of the Jordan, from the place where the priests' feet stood, carry them over with you, and lay them down in the place where you camp tonight.'" Then Joshua summoned the twelve men from the Israelites, whom he had appointed, one from each tribe. Joshua said to them, "Pass on before the ark of the LORD your God into the middle of the Jordan, and each of you take up a stone on his shoulder, one for each of the tribes of the Israelites, so that this may be a sign among you. When your children ask in time to come, 'What do those stones mean to you?' then you shall tell them that the waters of the Jordan were cut off in front of the ark of the covenant of the LORD. When it crossed over the Jordan, the waters of the Jordan were cut off. So these stones will be to the Israelites a memorial forever."

Those twelve stones, which they had taken out of the Jordan, Joshua set up in Gilgal, saying to the Israelites, "When your children ask their parents in time to come, 'What do these stones mean?' then you shall let your children know, 'Israel crossed over the Jordan here on dry ground.' For the LORD your God dried up the waters of the Jordan for you until you crossed over, as the LORD your God did to the Red Sea, which he dried up for us until we crossed over, so that all the peoples of the earth may know that the hand of the LORD is mighty, and so that you may fear the LORD your God forever" (Joshua 4:1-7; 20-24, NRSV).

CHAPTER 11

Step 8: Make Your Marriage Your Ministry

> I will bless those who bless you, and
> the one who curses you I will curse; and in you
> all the families of the earth shall be blessed.
> —Genesis 12:3, NRSV

Knowledge: The Sum of What Is Known

"All men [and women] by nature desire knowledge," said Aristotle, and Albert Einstein observed, "The only source of knowledge is experience." Although they were not recognized as marriage experts, Aristotle and Einstein contribute simple quotes that speak volumes for marriage.

Authenticity in your marriage requires knowledge born of experience. This experience comes from working through the previous ROCKS of redemption, offering, and covenant. As you've taken meaningful steps toward moving your marriage along its purpose-driven path, you have matured in your knowledge of God, of your spouse, and of yourself. Experience has shown you your areas of strength as well as weakness. Experience has yielded insight into the strengths, weaknesses, and needs of your spouse. Experience has revealed God's unmerited favor toward your marriage, despite these strengths and weaknesses. These experiences are the foundation from which you can elevate your marriage to the next level—the level of ministry. God desires your marriage to be a light that directs others to him. The next two chapters will provide you the insights to do just that. African

American marriages need mentors and cheerleaders. As you read, think, dialogue, and pray through the remainder of this book, I pray the Spirit will show you exactly how God intends to transform your knowledge into ministry.

The knowledge that comes from experience can transform your marriage into the dream of mutuality you've long desired. But, here is the catch: God desires more. Despite all you've learned, your experience remains incomplete until you give your knowledge to others. Jesus instructed his disciples that his investment in them was not only for them. In Matthew 28:19-20, Christ reveals his intent for our knowledge: to go and make disciples by teaching them obedience to God's commands. This Scripture, known as the Great Commission, is the ultimate power of your marriage. Your experiences in marriage shape your ability to bring others to God. Your knowledge is your power. The story of Harvey and Dorothy, a middle-aged couple with adult children, highlights the power of knowledge for personal and community transformation.

When Harvey and Dorothy were wed two years ago, it was the second marriage for each of them. But, they have been married to each other for twenty-six years total, having been previously married to one another, divorced, and remarried. Their first marriage was a nightmare, mostly due to Harvey's alcoholism and infidelity. Harvey was not physically abusive, but when he drank, he was a very poor decision-maker, especially when it came to flirting with other women. For years, Dorothy's own insecurities caused her to blame herself for Harvey's erratic behavior. Finally, after overhearing Harvey on the cell phone arranging to meet another woman, Dorothy became angry enough to file for divorce. They had been divorced for almost two years when Harvey called Dorothy to tell her that his life had been transformed. He had entered an alcohol treatment program and had been clean for more than a year. He had also become a Christian through the witness of his Alcoholics Anonymous sponsor. Although initially suspicious, Dorothy eventually agreed to reconnect with Harvey. Today, Harvey and Dorothy tell their amazing story of redemption, offering, and covenant to anyone who will listen, at their church and in the small group that they host for couples in troubled marriages.

In Joshua's vignette, the nation of Israel was at a significant crossroads. Faced with yet another seemingly insurmountable obstacle, the nation looked toward their new leader, Joshua. God had taken Moses, the leader who had brought them out of Egypt to the brink of the land that had been promised to their ancestors since the days of Abraham. Ahead of them lay the Jordan River and the plain of Jericho. The Jordan was a swift river at that time of year. Given the magnitude of the loss of Moses and the overwhelming obstacles they faced, the nation was confused and frightened about what to do next. And, even if they did find a way across the Jordan—then what?

The plains were guarded by the legendary city of Jericho. Its towering, five-hundred-year-old walls were a staggering deterrent to any Israelite attempt to take the remainder of God's Promised Land. Joshua understood that the enemy held the territory that God had promised him. God strategically had placed the Promised Land at the geographic center of a major trade route, a location that would maximize the world's exposure to the God of the Hebrews. By elevating a small agrarian nation to a position of strength, every major world culture would have to reckon with them. God wanted the world to know him through the works and faith of these, his people. The next step in this plan is recorded in Joshua 4, when God honors the faith and obedience of Joshua and the Hebrew nation by damming the Jordan River to allow the nation to cross.

Upon orchestrating the miraculous, God instructs Joshua to set up a memorial to that miracle. The monument was to memorialize two issues:

- That the world may know the power of God to do the "impossible."
- That the people of God may identify themselves as God-fearers.

God told Joshua that the miracle of the Jordan crossing was only the beginning of the promise. This advice can guide you to the next step in your marriage as well. God instructs Joshua to go into the middle of the Jordan—a symbol we'll interpret here as going to the heart of an experience—and to extract memorials that will be testimonies to the world about the power of God. Why would God command this, in light of the fact that he had already performed the miracle? The nation is already awed by yet another display of God's providence. Joshua has already proven that he is capable of continuing the legacy of Moses by being a vessel for the miracles of God. What more needs to happen?

God instructs Joshua to have twelve representatives (one from each tribe) return to the middle of the now-dry Jordan River bed and pick up twelve rocks to memorialize the miraculous. Further, God informs them that this exercise is specifically designed to foster knowledge among three sets of people: their children, the people of the world, and within themselves.

That Your Children May Know

In Chapter 1, we discussed the distorted views that many African American children and youth have about marriage, such as the idea that marriage is only for white people. Few of the black family structures around them show positive models of marriage. Our African American children need you. It is no wonder that God's first reason for the miracle at the Jordan is about the children, for it is the children who must carry the traditions for generations.

God says that a time will come when succeeding generations will inquire as to the meaning of these rocks. When they ask, the Hebrew people are to tell the story about what God did that day. God uses this oral tradition not only to educate them but to provide insight into his plan to influence the faith development of generations to come, including ours.

Your family of origin plays an integral role in your view of marriage. Your successes and struggles are related to your experiences with your parents. In other words, our knowledge (for better or worse) about marriage has been influenced by the stories lived and told by our parents, grandparents, other family members, and other key people in our development. This is precisely why Scripture admonishes us as Christian parents to train our children in the ways of the Lord—because as they develop, they will remember.

Unfortunately, many adult children marry having never received the seeds of promise. As children, we may have watched and listened with dismay as our parents and grandparents battled their demons of anger and fear, causing them to sow seeds of neglect, abandonment, and divorce in us. We watched and lived stories of discord. The sad reality of the sins of the parents visiting on the sixth and seventh generations means that, despite your best efforts, you may recreate many of these negative experiences in your own marriages—fostering a distorted knowledge base that impedes authentic connection with God.

However, God's hope comes in the form of the knowledge that holds the power to deliver your children from the generational struggles, bondages, and curses that you have battled. As your children watch you climb the ROCKS of marriage, God wants you to tell them. Imagine the power that Harvey and Dorothy's marriage journey has for their children. Their children, who are now adults, have seen a firsthand transformation from "messed to blessed." When they experience their own marriage challenges, they can be encouraged by not only the words but also the deeds of their parents. They will witness Christ's power to raise the dead (marriage) to life.

I believe that many African American Christian parents often frustrate the faith development of our children in this area. We errantly believe that we should shield our children from the struggles of marriage, thereby "protecting" them. We fail to tell them the mistakes that almost destroyed everything that we hold dear; we are leery of sharing the pains and disappointments that characterize many of our marital relationships. Some of us may be, understandably, too ashamed of our pasts to share them with our children.

> **While there are definite boundaries of privacy and appropriateness to observe depending on our children's ages, we must find ways to share about the miracles that God has done.**

While there are definite boundaries of privacy and appropriateness to observe depending on our children's ages, we must find ways to share about the miracles that God has done. God tells us in the book of Joshua that when our children ask about this memorial of rocks, we are to tell them about the miracle that took place here. Your children will only understand the miracle if they first understand the mess. Your testimonies of how God's hand in your marriage transformed your messes into miracles will establish the foundation of your children's marriages in the years ahead.

Conversely, that which you withhold out of shame or protection will also contribute to the blueprint of their marriages. As any family therapist will tell you, family secrets often become "told" through their expression in subsequent generations, because the light has not been shined to dispel the darkness.

Therefore, by telling the story of your marriage to your children, you help them understand that marital harmony is not ready-made like on television, but that it is work that is eternally successful only when God is in the middle of it. You give your children an astonishing gift of knowledge, not by being models of perfection, but by being living memorials to redemption. This, they will remember and live out in their own lives.

GOD INDICATES to Joshua that the memorial of twelve stones represents God's desire that future generations understand the miracle at the Jordan River. Think over the miracles that have happened or that need to happen in your marriage. Write down some practical things you can do to show, tell, and encourage future generations about God's provision, even in seemingly impossible circumstances.

That the World May Know

God tells Joshua in verse 24 that the second purpose of the rock memorial is that all the people of the earth may know that the hand of the Lord is mighty; therefore, we see that the power of our testimony should not end in our homes. God's intent is for the miracles in our lives to serve as living memorials of his might. Your navigation of the rocks in your marriage can witness to other marriages that are on the rocks, providing them with a future and a hope.

Discouraged couples need to hear the miracles that God has performed for you. You are the clearest sign of God's power that many couples will ever see. Sometimes, an act as simple as telling a young couple the number of years that you have been married to the same person is a powerful testimony, because they may suspect you have lived through quite a bit of strife to achieve that milestone. If you have never considered divorce as a way out of your struggles, share the foundation that prevented you from considering it. If you were on the brink of divorce and found a way back, share what saved you. Examples abound as to how your marital experiences can be a blessing to the kingdom of God.

Harvey and Dorothy use their marriage journey as a testimony to the power of the Lord. They hold monthly meetings with other married couples to encourage them to work through their troubles. Although this was originally a ministry in their church, the need was so great that couples from all over the city have been part of their monthly fellowship at one point or another. They are now sought-after speakers at marriage retreats, because of the authenticity that couples sense in their story of renewal.

The world is hungry for answers that do not lie in this world. Yet, they look to talk show gurus and best-selling authors for solutions that can only be found in a God-centered spirituality. The secular world's paradigm focuses on building the power of the individual. God's paradigm for marriage focuses on the power of partnership as expressed by two dynamic, interdependent individuals.

Therefore, you are situated at a cultural crossroads, pointing in a direction that is contrary to personal fulfillment and individual rights. Life (and death) is in the power of your tongue (Proverbs 18:21). Satan prefers that your tongue be silenced about what God has done for you and your marriage, trusting that your shame or guilt will guide your storytelling. As the world observes the miracles of transformation and liberation in your marriage, they will long to know the story, because we are all wired to seek such knowledge. This provides a wonderful opportunity to speak of the mighty power of the Lord as you share the absolute truth of the gospel message. Through this act of love shall your neighbors know that you are the Lord's disciple (John 13:35), speaking memorials that direct them to open their lives and their marriages to God.

That We May Know

God told the Hebrew nation to erect the memorial of rocks to liberate people within the family (the children) and outside the family (the world). But our God is an efficient God, and the power of our testimony comes full circle as we, ourselves, benefit. Much of the maturity that I possess in marriage is a direct result of having invested in the marriages of others. As I sit with couples and witness their pain, God shows me the areas in which I must minister to my own wife's pain. By actively listening to the frustration of others, I am better able to recognize and voice my own frustrations. We are called to be wounded healers—using our personal experiences of brokenness to heal relationships among others.

So many people make the mistake of standing on the sidelines, waiting for their marriages to be great, before they feel any responsibility or ability to minister to others. I challenge you to find even one example in Scripture where this is the case. Outside of Jesus, you will not find one. Why? Because this is not God's way; your investment in others is *part* of your healing. This is why discovering God's purpose for your marriage cannot end with redemption, offering, and covenant, which happen within you and between you and your partner. As you share your knowledge with others, you continue the healing process within yourself. Harvey and Dorothy would tell you the same thing. Their ministry to couples benefits them more than anyone else. They become more trusting and loving of each other as they witness the power of knowledge.

God tells Joshua that this memorial of the miracle is to imprint forever the fear of the Lord God into their minds. Despite discouragement, serial crises, shaky resolve, and even believing your marriage to be forsaken by God, your marriage ROCKS also stand as memorials to the miraculous, as tangible witnesses that God rewards faithfulness. Your ability to narrate for others the mighty works that the Lord has done is directly associated with the power that you now have to move to the next level of faith in God.

I ROCK Exercises

Scripture Memorization: Genesis 12:3, NRSV

I will bless those who bless you, and the one who curses you I will curse; and in you all the families of the earth shall be blessed.

Contemplation

Respond to the following points of contemplation in your personal journal:

1. What experiences in your marriage have contributed most to your knowledge of God?
2. Joshua's faith enabled him to lead a nation through the mighty Jordan River. From your perspective, what obstacles stand in your way to God's promises for your marriage? What will it take to overcome these obstacles?

Integration

3. Guilt and shame often prevent us from feeling qualified to share our marriage journeys with others. In as detailed a manner as possible, write your feelings about what prevents you from sharing more about your marriage with others. When your list is complete, pray and ask the Lord to transform these feelings into faith steps.

We ROCK Exercises

Contemplation

1. God sent Joshua to the place where a miracle occurred to establish a memorial. What experiences in your marriage best reflect the power of God to do the impossible?
2. What can you do as a couple to share with your children the miracles that God has done in your marriage? If you do not have children, who in your sphere of influence should hear your personal testimony?

Integration

3. With each of the following people, share a story about your marriage in which God's hand was clearly evident:
   • someone under the age of eighteen,
   • someone who needs encouragement in his or her engagement or marriage,
   • someone who is experiencing marital distress.

CHAPTER 12

Step 9: Memorialize Your Marriage

Don't worry that children never listen to you;
worry that they are always watching you."
—Robert Fulghum

Claiming Your Territory

Satan holds the territory that has been promised to you, yet God desires to place your marriage at the cultural crossroads. God has situated your marital promised land to maximize the world's exposure to him. The enemy relies on you to walk with a spirit of mediocrity, arrogance, and fear in order to thwart God's plan. While the Lord is nudging you to push your marriage beyond your comfort zone, the enemy desires that you compromise. Just as the nation of Israel stared, hopeless, at an overflowing and fast-moving Jordan, we sometimes experience hopelessness in our relationships. God challenges us to face impossible situations by having faith.

These biblical words of encouragement challenge us to reframe the obstacles in our paths as stepping stones to a higher level of faith and trust in God. As with the Israelites, God wants your marriage to be positioned as a force with which everyone around you must reckon. The Lord promises to perform both the mundane and the miraculous, if you submit your relationship to God by climbing the marriage ROCKS, thus becoming for the whole world a testimony to God's power to create beauty from ashes. The Spirit's strength is most emphasized in the areas in which your marriage is weakest.

We have examined the ways in which God has called you to a journey toward spiritual, emotional, and sexual intimacy. This elevation is not simply for your marital satisfaction, although well-meaning people may lead you to believe so. Rather, God is moving your marriage to new territories in order to influence people in a way that you may not have considered. I call you to move off the banks and cross over your Jordan, thus fulfilling the spiritual growth that God has promised.

God, through the Word, tells us that knowledge is power. More specifically, God tells us that we, the children of God, perish because of our lack of knowledge. As we have explored in previous chapters, this knowledge provides a threefold power: first, to secure the Christian legacy of future generations; second, to instill encouragement into your communities; and finally, to strengthen your own faith walk as you continue to negotiate whatever marital stumbling stones may appear.

Sharing Knowledge

Joshua's obedience to God included his willingness to convince the tribes that achieving God's plan involved yet another act of faith. The gravity of the "Jordan crisis" was lessened by the fact that the Hebrews had the shared experience of God as One who delivers from oppressors (e.g., release from Egyptian enslavement), who controls the forces of nature (e.g., the parting of the Red Sea), and who provides food (e.g., manna from heaven). Accounts of God as Deliverer, Way-maker, and Provider were foundational to their oral tradition. God's miracles gave them their sense of being set apart and special; in fact, all Hebrews understood the tenets of Abraham's covenant, in which God unconditionally identifies the Hebrew people as his own. These shared stories fostered shared meaning, which strengthened them for this new act of faith.

Harvey and Dorothy's story gives us a concrete example of God as Deliverer—releasing them from the clutches of an addiction. God as Provider met Dorothy and Harvey's needs in the difficult days following the divorce. And, as Way-maker, God guided them, through the Holy Spirit, to rediscover their identities in ways that transform marriages all over the city.

As we have seen, the divine plan for bringing the world to God is built on the sharing of knowledge. God positioned the Hebrew nation geographically for this task, but this plan further required that they remain faithful to Yahweh while being exposed to pagan deities. Similarly, God desires that we as Christians share our own experiences of God as Deliverer, Way-maker, and Provider in the settings in which he strategically places us. This also requires that we maintain our solidarity as agents of truth. I believe that maximizing the power of our shared knowledge and experience is a three-step process: remembering, constructing, and telling.

Remembering

We often take the power of memories for granted; yet, our memories obviously serve a crucial role in how we experience the world around us. Brain researchers study the interplay between short-term and long-term memory that is necessary for optimal functioning. Despite the fundamental necessity of memory in leading a normal life, memory is fallible. Our experiences tend to fade over time if they are not rehearsed or if they were not dramatic enough.

As our creator, God is well aware of the frailties of our minds and our tendencies to forget or minimize the past. This is precisely why the Lord instructed the Hebrew people to build a memorial for the specific purpose of fostering their remembering of the miraculous events in their lives. God further desired to create national unity in this memorializing process and thus required that a representative from each tribe participate. By instituting this memorial, God placed a record in the oral tradition of the Hebrew people to remember his mighty works for hundreds of generations.

Likewise, we need to remember the demonstrations of God's power in our marriages. I remember so vividly when Dalia and I desired to have a second child but were told by the doctor that Dalia was in premature menopause—a circumstance that appeared to end our hopes for another child. Fortunately, God, rather than the physicians, had the last word. After many prayers, God saw fit to honor this desire of our hearts. Dalia became pregnant and ultimately birthed our daughter, Kyrsten. I remember the incident in the book of Joshua nearly every time that I pray with my daughter, when I vocalize to God my thanks for the miracle of her birth. I was so heartened recently when, upon hearing that some people do not believe in prayer, my young daughter replied, "Well, that is just silly, because I'm only here because of prayer." My wife and I will continue to be vocally thankful for the miracles of birth and remembering.

I give thanks for God's hand in our lives regularly for three reasons. First, I sincerely want God to hear my gratitude for my wonderful daughter. Second, I want my daughter to understand how God moved mountains to create her, despite what the experts of our culture dictated—a powerful faith lesson for my daughter to carry throughout her life. She knows that God is not constrained by the beliefs, understanding, and science of our culture. Third, the miracle of Kyrsten's birth is a reminder to me that God is a Deliverer, a Way-maker, and a Provider. The repetition of speaking thanks to the Lord centralizes God's faithfulness in my thinking and impacts the way that I experience the world around me. This is precisely the influence that God sought to have upon the Hebrew nation with the erection of the memorial to the Jordan crossing. Ultimately, this is the same objective that God has in mind for Harvey and Dorothy's marriage and for the millions of couples around the world just like them. God wants us to remember his mighty works.

LET YOUR MIND wander over your marriage's history as you tackle these Marriage ROCKS lessons. Write as many incidences as you can remember in your relationship that demonstrate the power of God. Give as much detail as you can recall. As you look back at these demonstrations of God's power, how does it make you feel about God as Way-maker, Provider, and Deliverer? Remembering is the key to creating shared knowledge and meaning in your sphere of influence.

Constructing

After removing the rocks from the Jordan, the Hebrew people were to use them to construct a memorial at Gilgal. The point of national unity cannot be understated here. God wanted the entire nation to be involved in the memorializing (knowing) process. Previously, the Hebrew people had acted like twelve tribes rather than as one nation as God in his wisdom preferred. The very process of constructing this memorial created unity by joining them in the shared knowledge and meaning of the event. This unity was crucial as they faced entry into a Promised Land inhabited by enemies who vastly outnumbered them.

> As a couple, your shared experiences will demonstrate God's power to others, so the manner in which you narrate your story is critical.

As a couple, your shared experiences will demonstrate God's power to others, so the manner in which you narrate your story is critical. A *narrative* is the combination of certain facts plus the meaning we make of them. For example, the undisputed facts that Dalia and I were told about conception (e.g., biological evidence of hormonal levels that supposedly made it impossible for us to have another child) are intertwined with our nonfactual but equally true shared belief that God performed a miracle.

Our constructed narrative, like yours, holds the power to strengthen couples to meet the threats of the enemy. Further, your stories not only deliver others but remind you that God promises to do abundantly more in your marriage than he has already done. The very process of constructing these stories together brings you and your spouse closer; in fact, I have a therapist colleague who insists during premarital counseling that the couple narrate their story, because she believes the story that carries a couple to the altar is the same story they'll draw on during their inevitable future difficulties.

This premarital narrative is important because, frequently, the narrative that receives the most air time after the wedding is the problem narrative, the areas of your marriage in which you struggle and the reasons you believe this to be so. These problem narratives can consume so much of your mental and physical energy that there is little time or interest remaining to focus on the more positive aspects of your marriage. But, I believe this emphasis is exactly backward. We need to spend more time in conversation about the strengths, blessings, and miracles in our marriages to correct our natural inclination to focus on weaknesses. Conversation between spouses, particularly when focused on shared meaning and knowledge, is a bridge to couple unity. Unity in your marriage now is just as vital as unity was for the Hebrews as they crossed the Jordan into the land of their enemies.

Satan has targeted marriage. He knows that if he can destroy this most fundamental relationship that he can negatively impact generations of your family. Many of the disturbing narratives that we hear about the irrelevance of marriage in the African American community are prime examples of how Satan has had some success in his strategy to destabilize marriage for generations. You must refuse to be hoodwinked by Satan's offerings. Discovering authentic meaning in marriage requires that we are mindful of the stories of deliverance and provision in our marriages, in order to strengthen our relationships with God, with our partners, and with those who are looking to us for inspiration.

Telling

It is not enough to remember the work of God in our lives; we must construct a narrative that connects the hopelessness of our sinful state to the mercy of God in granting unmerited favor. This transition from hopelessness to hope is the heart of the gospel message. It is the shared experience of all who come to accept the Lord Jesus Christ as Savior. As important as personal salvation is, it is only one part of God's command to us. God commands us to spread the gospel message to the outermost parts of the earth. We must tell our neighbors about Christ's work of salvation.

The memorial of the Jordan River crossing is to serve as a visible reminder for the Israelites to tell their descendents exactly what God did there. It is difficult to imagine where we would be if God's miracles were lost in human history. Fortunately, we have the Bible, which is the most-read book in the world. But, your Christian life may be the only "Bible" that many people will ever see; yet, we hesitate to open our lives so that others may read God's story in us. Simply put, we have too many untold miracles in our lives to remain closed. How many untold testimonies lie within you? I dare you to count them.

> **We have become a Christian culture focused more on prayer requests than on prayers answered.**

As Christians, we live in a church culture in which it is commonplace to say that we are praying to the Lord for answers, often asking others to pray for us. Yet, we often fail to tell the many ways that God has answered those petitions. More to the point, once the petition has been made, we don't even notice the small answers received. We have become a Christian culture focused more on prayer requests than on prayers answered. Once God has answered one prayer, we often quickly move to the next prayer request on our lists, rather than praising and worshiping the Lord for previous miracles, however small they may be. This reflects a stance that is self-centered rather than God-centered. Advancing the knowledge of God's mighty works in our culture requires that we remember what the Lord has done already, construct a faith perspective and testimony narrative, and proclaim his works to everyone within our sphere of influence.

Our culture has more resources to communicate God's provision than ever before in human history. We have access to the Internet to tell our narratives via e-mail, websites, blogs, Internet radio, and social networking sites. We have unprecedented access to royalty-publishing and self-publishing houses to get our narrative testimonies into print. And, of course, we have more conventional channels to reach our church members, neighbors, and family. There is a whole world out there for you to tell about the power of God. What are you waiting for?

Regardless of the present state of your marriage, the complete answer to marriage lies within you, simply because you have a powerful story to tell about how you started out at point A and arrived here today. This claim is not based on human power but rather on an understanding that God desires for you to be a conduit through which his mighty works are known.

I ROCK Exercises

Scripture Memorization: Hosea 4:6, NRSV

My people are destroyed for lack of knowledge; because you have rejected knowledge, I reject you from being a priest to me. And since you have forgotten the law of your God, I also will forget your children.

Contemplation

Respond to the following points of contemplation in your personal journal:

1. Think about the condition of marriages among your family and friends. In what ways might your marriage minister to them? What keeps you from doing more in this area?
2. How, if at all, does the idea of being a wounded healer in your marriage liberate you to more actively become a minister to other people's marriages?

Integration

3. Think back over the physical, psychological, and emotional wounds you have experienced in your life. Which biblical character (if you do not know biblical characters, choose a character from a movie or story) has experienced wounds most similar to yours in at least one of these areas? How, if at all, does this character's journey toward God inspire your own?

We ROCK Exercises

Contemplation

1. Think of one instance in which God has proven himself to be each of the following in your marriage: a Deliverer, a Way-maker, and a Provider.

2. God has proven himself faithful to you in the past. But, what does your marriage need most from him now in order to help the faith development of others?

Integration

3. As a couple, develop the story of your marriage. The emphasis of your story should be on the ways in which God has proven to be a Way-maker, Provider, and Deliverer in your own seemingly hopeless situations. Write this story in a single page. Who in your circle of friends and family might benefit from this knowledge of your experience with God?

PART SIX

Discovering Sacred Space: The Rock of Worship

It is only when people begin to worship that they begin to grow.
—CALVIN COOLIDGE

Congratulations! You have made it to the final plateau in the ascent toward authentic meaning in your marriage. I hope that you feel proud of this accomplishment. Of course, the real achievement lies in the journey that you embarked upon, hopefully alongside your spouse or spouse-to-be. My prayer is that you have not only discovered each other in a new way, but that your relationship with God has been enriched. Because this entire ROCKS method is ultimately about God, it is fitting that the final rock, sacred space, focuses on worship. Philosopher Immanuel Kant said, "The human heart refuses to believe in a universe without purpose." In the end, worship is the purpose of both our creation as individuals and our union as couples.

Jacob left Beer-sheba and went toward Haran. He came to a certain place and stayed there for the night, because the sun had set. Taking one of the stones of the place, he put it under his head and lay down in that place. And he dreamed that there was a ladder set up on the earth, the top of it reaching to heaven; and the angels of God were ascending and descending on it. And the LORD stood beside him and said, "I am the LORD, the God of Abraham your father and the God of Isaac; the land on which you lie I will give to you and to your offspring; and your offspring shall be like the dust of the earth, and you shall spread abroad to the west and to the east and to the north and to the south; and all the families of the earth shall be blessed in you and your offspring. Know that I am with you and will keep you wherever you go, and will bring you back to this land; for I will not leave you until I have done what I have promised you." Then Jacob woke from his sleep and said, "Surely the LORD is in this place— and I did not know it!" And he was afraid, and said, "How awesome is this place! This is none other than the house of God, and this is the gate of heaven!"

So Jacob rose early in the morning, and he took the stone that he had put under his head and set it up for a pillar and poured oil on the top of it. He called that place Bethel [house of God]; but the name of the city was Luz at the first. Then Jacob made a vow, saying, "If God will be with me, and will keep me in this way that I go, and will give me bread to eat and clothing to wear, so that I come again to my father's house in peace, then the LORD shall be my God, and this stone, which I have set up for a pillar, shall be God's house; and of all that you give me I will surely give one-tenth to you" (Genesis 28:10-22, NRSV).

CHAPTER 13

Step 10: Mobilize Your Marriage for Worship

Let the word of Christ dwell in you richly;
teach and admonish one another in all wisdom;
and with gratitude in your hearts sing psalms,
hymns, and spiritual songs to God.
—Colossians 3:16, NRSV

Sacred Space: A Place Set Apart for Worship

Worship is a central element of the African American experience. Our worship is energetic, soulful, and often a public demonstration of an inner commitment. The African American worship experience is unique. Christian researcher George Barna notes the centrality of worship to the black experience, saying that his research "found that the black church emphasis upon and facilitation of authentic worship is something that most people yearn for, but relatively few American churches successfully provide for their people."[1] With such a legacy, it should come as no surprise that black marriages hold such potential as sacred vessels.

What comes to your mind when you think of the word *sacred*? Grand cathedrals, ancient scrolls, the Bible? *Sacred* is not a common word in our vernacular. It invokes images of purity, of holiness, and of heaven. In its purest form, *sacred* refers to something that is set apart for worship. When you consider your church as sacred, you understand it as a place reserved for worshipping God. When you revere the Bible as sacred, it is because you worship

God through knowledge of the Scripture. In other words, the sacred is always about raising the Lord's banner and worshipping God. So, here is the question as we broach the capstone: Is your marriage sacred? Is your marriage relationship a channel through which you, your spouse, and others worship the Lord? God instituted the system of marriage as something sacred—he even compared it to his own relationship with the church! It is appropriate, therefore, to pose this question about the sacred quality of your marriage. When your marriage ROCKS, you are indeed raising a sacred banner over your relationship, your family, and your home, proclaiming, "But as for me and my household, we will serve the LORD" (Joshua 24:15, NRSV).

American culture has lost touch with the sacred. A concept that was central to previous generations, through Sabbath observation, reverence for holy living, and respect for God's creation, is now marginally important. Our pursuits of entertainment, leisure, and sheer fun leave little room for it. As Christians, we have carved out a neat space to prioritize the sacred—most often Sunday morning between 10 a.m. and noon, though admittedly much of our Sunday worship also resembles entertainment these days. Even in the highly religious, church-attending African American culture, the distinction between the sacred and the temporal continues to blur.

Reaching the pinnacle of *Marriage ROCKS*, demands a broader examination of the sacred in your life. Through your reading of this book and the circumstances that God is arranging in your life, God is summoning you to a wider view of sacred space. This broader perspective includes not only places, but also people and things that are set apart to worship him. Read the story of Malachi and Cissy to see how this broader view of the sacred has mobilized their marriage into a ministry that has impacted hundreds of families affected by incarceration.

Malachi and Cissy have been married for six years. However, they were separated for nearly two years when Malachi served time in a minimum-security prison for tax evasion. In prison,

Malachi had a lot of time to think about the mistakes that he had made in life and about his future with Cissy. While working in the laundry center one day, Malachi had a conversation with a fellow inmate named Johnny that changed the course of Malachi's life. Johnny, serving three years, confided to Malachi that his wife wanted a divorce because she could no longer deal with waiting for his release and she'd realized that she no longer loved him. Johnny became clinically depressed and made an unsuccessful suicide attempt. During Cissy's visit that weekend, Malachi showed her the rough outline of a nonprofit ministry that he wanted them to develop together. Its focus would be on engaged and married couples in which one or both spouses are or have been incarcerated.

Although skeptical, Cissy agreed to think about it. After Malachi's release, he and Cissy enrolled in a marriage and family therapy program at a local university. Today, their organization, Living Just-Us, has touched the lives of more than five hundred couples by offering relationship education and counseling services within several jails and prisons in surrounding cities. They credit God with the vision and for using it to heal the emotional wounds in their marriage and for bringing them back into intimate fellowship with him.

Malachi and Cissy's ministry has transformed the loneliness and emptiness of prison life into a time of purposeful reflection that provides connection points between spouses. In other words, couples involved in Living Just-Us have a space to demonstrate their love and commitment to one another, despite their physical separation. In their subtle, compassionate way, Malachi and Cissy pray for and communicate the love of Christ to these couples.

As you read the final chapters of *Marriage ROCKS*, pray that the Lord opens your eyes, just as he did Malachi and Cissy's, so you can see your marriage as sacred space infused with God's presence. Also, pray that God divinely positions your marriage to create sacred spaces in the paths that you tread—sacred communities set apart for worship.

Revisiting Jacob

In this final rock, sacred space, we return to the story of Jacob to help us with the last stage of our climb. We last saw Jacob erecting a monument of rocks at Mizpah, and we now find him journeying back to his homeland after departing from the home of his father-in-law, Laban. Jacob's transformation has already begun, but apparently God has more in mind. While Jacob lies sleeping in the open air upon the hard ground one night, God comes to him in the dream widely known as "Jacob's Ladder." In this dream, Jacob sees angels ascending and descending upon a ladder that reaches from the earth to the heavens with God himself positioned at the top. God speaks in the dream, identifying himself with Jacob's ancestors, Abraham and Isaac. God is encouraging Jacob to recognize that the power God showed his ancestors is also available for him.

Why does Jacob need such encouragement? He needs encouragement because his identity has been shaken, to say the least, after thirteen years away from home and being embroiled in constant rivalry with his uncle Laban. How would his family receive him following his deception and flight? No longer secure in the promises God had decreed for him as a young child, he needs to remember his destiny. More to the point, he needs to be reminded of the One who is the Creator of destiny.

The Power of a Dream

Have you ever awakened from a dream feeling caught between the real and the imagined? Some people today dismiss dreams as psychological artifacts, unbridled anxiety, or maybe just the result of going to bed too soon after eating. Jacob, the product of a culture that respected dreams, understood their power. He was, in fact, so overwhelmed by the Lord's presence that, when he awakened, he was certain that the very spot upon which he lay must be the gateway to heaven. How could this place—one that almost literally captures "caught between a rock and a hard place"—possibly be a gateway to heaven?

Further, I can imagine the discomfort in Jacob's sleeping arrangement. Although sleeping in the open night air on the ground with a rock as a pillow might appeal to a few outdoor enthusiasts, I suspect most of us would have had a pretty restless night. Yes, Jacob was lying in a hard place—but this is what makes his reaction even more amazing. Jacob proclaims that the Lord must surely be in this place, a fact about which he claims previous ignorance. At first glance, Jacob appears to be suggesting that the Lord must inhabit the physical place where he lay. While this would be accurate, the Lord is doing more here than even Jacob realizes.

Much to Jacob's surprise, this dream was an unanticipated spiritual encounter. His exclamation about the Lord's presence not only refers to this geographical place, but to Jacob's own spiritual growth. Jacob is right—he did not even realize the Lord was there. Jacob's journey of spiritual emptiness made him ignorant of the fact that God was continually present with him.

But here in this hard place with a rock for a pillow, Jacob's experience of God is reassured. "Surely the LORD is in this place" is spoken with awe. His spiritual eyes are gradually opening to the reality that God's presence is with him wherever his feet tread.

Thus, when Jacob rises in the morning, he takes his rock-pillow and anoints it as a sacred house of God—a place of worship. What a glorious image of how God transforms hard places to sacred spaces! Of course, Jacob's circumstances had not changed, but his spiritual eyes were now open to the presence of God.

GOD OPENED Jacob's spiritual eyes to reaffirm his identity as an agent of blessing and change in his culture. During your journey through the *Marriage ROCKS* program, what has God shown you about your identity and purpose: (1) as an individual, (2) as a marriage partner, and (3) as a neighbor in community? Note your responses, give some examples in each area, and write

how you feel about your responses (e.g., excited, worried, fearful). The Spirit wants to transform all of these areas into places that are set apart for God.

How open are your spiritual eyes concerning your marriage? The exercises at the end of Chapters 13 through 15 will help crystallize your marriage's spiritual goals—mainly by helping you outline a Marriage Ministry Plan (MMP) as a couple. The MMP outline is a roadmap to guide your thinking about how your gifts and passions create sacred space that blesses and empowers others.

Through the course of this book, you and your spouse have redeemed each other and increased emotional intimacy. As you have actively engaged in these steps, I am confident that your marriage has achieved a level occupied by relatively few others—a monument to the power of God. The next step is to distribute this power so that hard places, through Jacob-like "aha" moments, are transformed to sacred spaces.

Think about electricity for a moment. Millions of watts of power are available, thanks to modern technology. But, what if there were no electrical power lines transporting this current? Then all of this available power would remain untapped. Such is the case with your marriage. If you do not distribute the power generated by your authentic marriage for the purpose of illuminating your neighbor, you stymie what God desires to do through you. In a real sense, you limit how much your marriage grows and evolves.

Regardless of how strong your marriage is now, God can make it even better. Why not offer yourselves by telling your story to others? Go ahead. Step into faith by stepping outside your comfort zone. As you climb this final stone, you will recognize the potential for your marriage to become one of your most effective forms of ministry. As we dissect Jacob's dream, we will discern the principles that testify to God's power to cultivate the sacred spaces of ministry through your marriage.

I ROCK Exercises

Scripture Memorization: Colossians 3:16, NRSV

Let the word of Christ dwell in you richly; teach and admonish one another in all wisdom; and with gratitude in your hearts sing psalms, hymns, and spiritual songs to God.

Contemplation

Respond to the following points of contemplation in your personal journal:

1. How does the story of Jacob's ladder relate to your marriage?
2. How important is it for you to see your marriage as a sacred space? What makes this difficult?

Integration

3. Over the next two chapters, you will be developing the outline of a ministry plan for your marriage. The first step is to brainstorm where your personal passions lie. Begin your planning process by considering the following list of settings where you might serve with your spouse. Rank each on a scale of one to seven, where one is "Not at all passionate" and seven is "Extremely passionate" about working in each scenario:

Crisis situations	Job/career development
Financial stewardship	Elder care
Parenting skills	Hospice care
Spiritual formation	Incarcerated/Ex-offenders
Relationship education	Bible studies
Bereavement (grief and loss)	Other

We ROCK Exercises

Contemplation

1. How can you and your spouse better distribute the power that you have accumulated as authentic marriage partners?
2. For whom has your marriage become a gateway to heaven?

Integration

3. Compare your personal responses to the third "I ROCK" exercise. Identify areas where your interests and passions are most similar. Discuss ideas for how you as a couple can reach out to these people. Incorporate each of your perspectives in this brainstorming process. Throughout these discussions, be prayerful individually and as a couple to discern God's will for your ministry.

CHAPTER 14

Step 11: Anoint Your Marriage as Sacred

Love's greatest gift is its ability to
make everything it touches sacred.
—BARBARA DE ANGELIS

In the last chapter, I asked you whether you think your marriage is sacred. Is it set aside to worship God? Jacob's dream shows that any place on earth that God touches is sacred; therefore, if you endeavor to make your marriage godly, then it is also sacred. Let's examine these principles, so that you may understand the ways your relationship is already sacred, and that you may learn to build on that understanding.

Principle #1: Your Ministry Is a Bridge between the Earth and the Divine

Jacob's dream illustrates two of the unchanging attributes of God—omnipresence and omnipotence. God is everywhere at the once, and God encompasses all power. Nevertheless, every married couple experiences seasons of wondering, "Where is God?" The Lord may feel distant. Cissy, the wife in the previous chapter, often talks about her anger toward God while Malachi was in prison. Even happily married couples question God's presence when life's circumstances and relationship challenges cause disappointment. Others, like Malachi, may not question God's presence but in their pain no longer believe God's power is available to them when they need it most—such as when they are behind prison bars.

The story of Jacob's ladder provides reassurance that God's power and presence are, in fact, accessible to us. As God stands atop the ladder, so does his supremacy stand over the matters of this world. Further, the ministering angels, who are divinely commissioned to traverse this ladder between God and Jacob's uncomfortable place, are also reassuring you: Any place God touches on earth is indeed sacred. Malachi, buoyed by the biblical stories of imprisoned heroes such as Joseph, Paul, and Silas, encourages the incarcerated that when God touches the prison, that place is sacred ground.

In a recent conversation with one of my church's ministers about the prison ministry in which he has been involved for many years, I clearly saw Malachi's point. There is a tremendous opportunity for us as African Americans, particularly as we are disproportionately incarcerated, to transform prison grounds to sacred spaces of redemption and healing. The hundreds of prisoners flocking to the weekly worship services is evidence of God's touch—through the willingness of some individuals to distribute the power and authority God has given them.

Hebrews 1:14 asks, "Are not all angels spirits in the divine service, sent to serve for the sake of those who are to inherit salvation?" (NRSV). In other words, even in his supremacy, God will minister to you personally. The ladder that extends from heaven to earth is a vehicle of God's power—not temporal and fleeting power but divine power, power with transformative properties. God provides access to his power so that you can become a sort of an electrical transfer station, connecting the promises of heaven with the needs of people on earth.

As you allow God to continue to transform your marriage, you are empowered as his agent in your sphere of influence. As you share your testimony of redemption and offering, you will be a living example to others that God is indeed an ever-present help in the time of trouble (Psalms 46:1). Through your stories of marital covenant, you will remind others that God will never leave or forsake them (Joshua 1:5). Your marriage ushers the sacred into the difficult situations as your story invokes worship of the power of God.

Principle #2: Your Ministry Speaks to Every Corner of the World

The second principle of Jacob's dream speaks to the breadth of possibility for your ministry. Remember, Acts 1:8 tells us, "But you will receive power when the Holy Spirit has come upon you; and you will be my witnesses in Jerusalem, in all Judea and Samaria, and to the ends of the earth" (NRSV). God gives you power so that you can be a witness to his glory, and he clearly desires that your influence transcend your own home, city, and even surrounding cities. God instructs the newly empowered saints to go beyond Jerusalem, Judea, and Samaria. With the power they now possess, they are to push to the very ends of the known world.

Even before this New Testament advent of the Holy Spirit, God conveys the same message to Jacob. In our vignette, God tells Jacob that his descendents will spread in every direction as a source of blessing to the earth. Just as the electrical power gets distributed from its source by electrical lines that transfer the current, God's display of power on earth is optimized as God's people are available to transfer the current.

The universal appeal of marriage makes it an ideal ministry opportunity. Malachi and Cissy will never see the ultimate reach of their ministry. They have personally ministered to approximately five hundred couples. But, how many others have these five hundred couples influenced through their participation in Living Just-Us? We cannot ultimately know. But, we can be assured that generations of marriages and families will survive (and thrive in) the challenge of incarceration, because of how God positioned this ministry to a neglected and ostracized population.

People around the world are interested in the purpose of their marriage. I am amazed at the inquiries that I receive from Africa, India, and the Far East through the Discovering Family International website at http://www.discoverfamily.org. Your marriage, because of your missteps and failures, believe it or not, models hope to every place you tread as you lift the Lord up from the earth, that God will draw all people to himself (John 12:32)—the epitome of what it means to create sacred space.

Principle #3: Your Ministry Is the Embodiment of God's Presence

God communicated a remarkable vision to Jacob about the amount of influence that he and his descendents would have on this earth. At the end of the dream, the angel assures Jacob that God is with him as Jacob works toward all that God has promised him. God wants Jacob to understand that the challenges before him are not too large for God. Yes, the task is big, but God is bigger. The Holy Spirit will cover you when you walk in God's promise.

We tend to experience God most powerfully when exercising our gifts for him through ministry.

How do you know when God is with you? That answer is simple—God is always with you. Perhaps the question should be—when do you *feel* God is with you? Unfortunately, this question cannot be answered so quickly. I feel God's presence most when I am confident and humbled that I am doing what God has gifted me to do. Malachi and Cissy say that they most feel God's presence when the incarceration ends and the couple joyfully reunite. This couple has the determination to make a solid commitment to implement a change to their marriage. Many of us would agree that God's presence is most strongly felt when we use our God-given talents and desires for a God-ordained purpose. Phrased another way, we tend to experience God most powerfully when exercising our gifts for him through ministry. As the Olympic athlete Eric Liddell said memorably in the film *Chariots of Fire*, "I believe God made me for a purpose, but he also made me fast. And when I run, I feel his pleasure."

As we minister in obedience to the Lord, using our gifts and availability, we create sacred space around us—because our ministries are the embodiment of God's presence on earth.

YOUR MARRIAGE is anointed as sacred as you accept and adopt the three principles. We most feel God's presence when we operate within the talents and purpose he has given us. In what ways do you see these principles applied in your marriage? If you do not see some of them right now, in what ways would you like to see these principles manifested in your marriage? Praise God for what you see and for what you desire to see.

Anointing Your Marriage as Sacred Space

When Jacob arose in the morning following his dream, he set his rock-pillow upright, transforming the pillow to a pillar. He anointed it with oil, declaring that spot (and his life) to be Bethel, the house of God. Further, Jacob committed himself and his descendents to worship God in that place. You mark sacred space in your marriage when you memorialize your hard places as well as your comfortable places as worthy of praise—transforming those stumbling stones to standing stones. Jacob's dream came from a place of desperation. By morning, God had transformed it into a place of worship. I am reminded of the words of David, "Weeping may linger for the night, but joy comes with the morning" (Psalm 30:5, NRSV). We continue to discover the house of God when we receive God as our advocate in the dark places in life, including in our marriages.

Jacob's dream does not belong only to him. It is the reality for all believers. Like Jacob, we risk missing God's presence simply because we don't feel him. The ministering angels traversing Jacob's ladder are surrounding you right now, even as you read these words! Whether or not your place is comfortable, take a moment to thank God for attending angels.

We naturally strive for the comfortable. However, Jacob's continued transformation seems to have required discomfort, so I ask: Are God's purposes, most fully grasped in our places of discomfort? Are our minds and hearts most open to him in our despair, because our human means have been exhausted?

Can you imagine your home as Bethel? Anoint your home as the house of God—literally. Say a blessing over a bottle of oil. Physically anoint every room in your home with a prayer and a cross of oil. Pray for God to transform your place into a power station that connects heaven and earth, that influences everyone who enters it toward holiness. Pray that it radiates God's presence. Remember, a key element of Jacob's epiphany is the realization that it is not only the geographical place that is the gateway to heaven. He was himself becoming a gateway to heaven. Malachi and Cissy have become gateways to heaven. As you have embarked on this journey through *Marriage ROCKS*, so are you. After you have anointed your home, take the next step. Anoint each other, emphasizing your submission to the three transforming principles found in Jacob's dream: to be a bridge for God, to be willing to extend this bridge through the ends of the earth, and to be the presence of God to whomever he puts in your path.

As you submit to these steps, you provide a portal through which God pours blessings. That which previously seemed impossible now feels possible. Entrenched patterns of distrust and disrespect begin to overturn. The intimacy for which you have longed sparks anew.

Let's be clear. There is no magic wand or silver bullet to finding this sacred marriage sanctuary. Discovering sacred space in your marriage is a commitment to the pursuit of God's purposes in your marriage—an endeavor that prioritizes worshipping the Lord.

I ROCK Exercises

Scripture Memorization: Acts 1:8, NRSV

But you will receive power when the Holy Spirit has come upon you; and you will be my witnesses in Jerusalem, and in all Judea and Samaria, and to the ends of the earth.

Contemplation

Respond to the following points of contemplation in your personal journal:

1. This chapter's first principle relates to how God desires ministry to connect heaven and earth. What can you personally do to become a better "ladder" for distributing God's power? What will it take for you to make this commitment?
2. This chapter's second and third principles advocate a broad perspective, recognizing the many ministry opportunities that exist. Based on the ideas that you generated in the last chapter, brainstorm some specific ministry ideas of interest that would stretch your marriage out of your comfort zone, if you were to do them. Think outside the box.

Integration

3. Jacob's discomfort helped him to see God's presence. How might the discomforts and difficulties that you have experienced in your marriage help you engage people in the areas of ministry that you and your spouse are considering? Be as specific as possible.

We ROCK Exercises

Contemplation

1. How can you better distribute the power you have accumulated as authentic partners?
2. In this chapter you anointed your home as a house of God. As a couple, discuss how you expect and desire this anointing to change the way you interact with each other.

Integration

3. In the previous chapter, you prioritized areas of ministry in which you could work as a couple. Given your response to this chapter's contemplation exercises, research and identify at least three public or private organizations near you that currently serve this population. If no one serves this population, what steps would be necessary to begin such a ministry? Contact one of these organizations within the next week to learn more. On a related note, if you are currently meeting with a

Marriage ROCKS small group, your group may also be in the planning process for a group project. The group project should be considered a separate project from the one you and your spouse develop together. If you are not currently meeting with a *Marriage ROCKS* small group, pray about either joining or starting one. The *Marriage ROCKS* leader's guide can help you get started.

CHAPTER 15

Step 12: Cultivate Communities of Belonging

Testimony is an integral part of the Black religious tradition. It is the occasion where the believer stands before the community of faith in order to give account of the hope that is in him or her.
—James Cone

Over the last two chapters, you have been reading and thinking about the ways in which your marriage is set apart as an instrument of worship—set apart for God. The electricity power grid has been compared to the manner in which God has empowered your marriage as a conduit for ministry. For all of our metaphors and biblical vignettes to make the case, we must always remain centered on a single point: Becoming a power station for God is really all about Jesus. Jesus is the embodiment of sacred space; every place he touches becomes a sacred space. As Malachi and Cissy have shown, even prison cells can be holy ground. Therefore, as you invite Jesus into your marriage, the opportunities for influence and worship are limitless.

Climbing Jesus' Ladder

In John 1:43-51, we find a powerful story about Nathanael that will inform our connection between Jacob's experience and Jesus' ministry. Take a few moments right now to grab your Bible and read this passage.

Nathanael, like many contemporary Christians, doubted the authenticity of Jesus, although he was sincere in his desire to find the Messiah. When Jesus approached Nathanael, he told Nathanael he had seen him sitting underneath the fig tree. The fig tree was recognized among the Jews as a metaphor for a place of meditation. Nathanael is awed by Jesus' words, because Nathanael was convinced that there was no one around to have seen this. Nathanael was sure that Jesus could only have seen him through some supernatural means, thus prompting him to believe Jesus must actually be the Messiah that Jesus claimed to be. Jesus responded, "Do you believe because I told you that I saw you under the fig tree? You will see greater things than these," adding, "Very truly, I tell you, you will see heaven opened and the angels of God ascending and descending upon the Son of Man" (John 1:50-51, NRSV). Does the phrase *ascending and descending* sound familiar? The imagery is exactly the same as the description of the dream experienced by Jacob hundreds of years earlier.

Jesus takes the Old Testament passage of Jacob's ladder (with which Nathanael, as a devout Jew, would have been very familiar) and substitutes himself for the ladder. In other words, Jesus tells Nathanael that, while Jacob saw angels ascending and descending upon a ladder, Nathanael will see angels ascending and descending upon Jesus. God previously used Jacob's ladder as the connection of blessing between heaven and earth, but God now uses his Son, Jesus, as the conduit for his blessings. But, Jesus' lesson does not end there. Jesus' description of himself as "Son of Man" is also important, because it highlights the humanity of Christ. Why is the humanity of Christ important here? It demonstrates that Jesus is indeed the model for all of humanity. As we accept him as our Savior and walk in his power, by association, we become the conduits of blessing between heaven and earth for those around us.

Further, Jesus' words to Nathanael speak to the critical role of marriage in our culture. Immediately after Jesus reveals himself as the ladder connecting the blessings of God to earth, Jesus performs his first public miracle at the wedding in Cana. Is it coincidence that this transforming of water into wine takes place at a wedding? We will have to ask the Lord that one when we meet him! For now, I am satisfied to know that God, through Jesus, is divinely revealing both the purpose of Jesus Christ and the opportunity found in marriage as ministry. Jesus came to take our ordinary existence (water) and to transform it into the extraordinary (wine). Jesus came to transform our ordinary marriages into extraordinary ones. And, get this: Jesus' new wine was declared by the master of the wedding banquet to be superior in quality to the wine pressed by human hands! As Jesus transforms the ordinary places in your marriage, your marriage will be recognized as superior to all of the partial solutions to marital happiness that this world offers.

Discovering Your Ministry

The first step toward creating Bethel in your marriage is inviting Jesus to be its centerpiece. This entails more than accepting him as your personal Savior—although that is an important element. Rather, it involves serving the Lord with the skills, gifts, and passions that God has gifted to you and your spouse.

Using these talents to bless marriages and families in your community and beyond requires that you, through Jesus, become the ladder connecting heaven and earth. You become the means for blessing others, by introducing the Spirit of Christ into the people and organizations within your sphere of influence. It is useful to identify a space that is particular to your giftedness in which to minister to marriages. To this end, I suggest that you do three things: (1) know thyself; (2) abandon the one-size-fits-all approach to ministry; and, (3) cultivate communities of belonging.

Know Thyself

The ancient Greek aphorism "know thyself" captures a crucial element in the pursuit of marriage as ministry. Personality, skills, and interests rightly influence the ministry model that most resonates with you; your preferences in interacting with other people influence the manner in which you choose to minister within that model. There are many ways that you can gain a richer understanding of what works for you, including personality assessments, therapists, coaches, and asking those who know you. What is most important is that you find a space for ministry that suits you as individuals and as a couple.

Years ago, Dalia and I made a conscious decision to impact marriages for the kingdom of God. However, because we are so different from each other, our methods of impact vary widely. I am more extroverted and enjoy teaching in front of audiences as well as writing in my office. Other times, I might be in a clinical milieu, counseling directly with a couple. Dalia's more introverted personality and preference for one-on-one dialogue led to distinctly different but no less passionate ministry expressions. Dalia ministers to marriage through her encouragement of wives and through sharing her experiences within the small-group context, where relationships are more personal. So, our approaches may differ from that of Malachi and Cissy, who together teach workshops and counsel families of the incarcerated. There is no one right way. It is about what works for your partnership while respecting your individuality.

Healthy Boundaries Create Sacred Space

Individual differences between partners can complicate feeling like a ministry team. I also believe Christian culture socializes us to think primarily about our individual ministries. So, even when we marry, we may continue to think ministerially as individuals rather than as partners. Marriage partnership as ministry obviously requires an examination of the space in which you are most comfortable and impactful as an individual. Once that has been accomplished, molding your individual styles into a unique team approach involves effort and negotiation. Admittedly, this is sometimes tough to do.

Dalia and I continue to struggle with this even as we move forward. For example, my spontaneity and procrastination are deeply engrained in my personality, as is my scientific style of analysis. Because I can easily calculate exactly how long it will take me to do a task to my standard of excellence, I will frequently procrastinate until I have just that amount of time left before starting the task. So, while it is fair to call me a planner of sorts, I would consider myself a spontaneous planner. Talk about driving my wife crazy!

Dalia is a methodical planner. Her ideal is to think about a task weeks ahead of its deadline, if not months ahead. She works steadily toward completing the task, allowing ample time to double-check everything. Talk about driving me crazy!

In some of our attempts to work together in marriage ministry, we have almost literally driven each other mad. It sometimes feels like we are on different wavelengths. Can you relate to this at all? Gradually, however, we are getting better at playing into our respective strengths and avoiding pressure to do things the way the other would.

> **HOW WELL** do you know yourself as it pertains to your ministry gifts? What is most exciting for you about ministering to others? What are your fears? How great is your capacity to sit with the failures, the struggles, and the victories of other couples? Have you ever discussed this with your spouse? Write down some of your thoughts about these questions.

I have noticed another fascinating dynamic to marriage ministry. The more you can become a container for others' painful marital experiences, the more positively your marriage will be influenced. I have no doubt that my journey to becoming an advocate for marriages around the world has had more impact on my marriage than I have had on anyone else's. I have become a more sensitive and compassionate husband and partner to my wife. You will never know the potential of your marriage until you give your marriage away.

Abandon the One-Size-Fits-All Approach

In the 1960s, anthropologist Edward Hall conducted research studies on how North Americans define the acceptable personal spaces that surround individuals. Generally, Hall found that human beings subconsciously interact in four spaces: intimate space (zero to eighteen inches), personal space (eighteen inches to four feet), social space (four feet to twelve feet), and public space (twelve or more feet). Hall coined the term *proxemics*, referring to the manner in which physical space influences interaction, meaning, and belonging.[1]

Based on Hall's work, author Joseph Myers, founder of Front-porch—an organization specializing in fostering conversations that promote and develop community—developed ministry models for Christian expression in each of these four spaces. He notes that people have different personalities and learning styles, and he suggests that God's people must foster a kingdom culture that enables a sense of belonging, what he calls *relational connection points*. His work is useful to our discussion here.

According to Myers, ministering in public space "isn't about connecting person-to-person as much as it is about sharing a common experience."[2] When I attend a conference with others who are interested in marriage and family ministry, we revel in our similar passion for supporting the institution of marriage. Our common experience inspires us that, as individuals, we belong to a transcendent movement. Public space ministry most typically happens in groups of twenty or more people.

Ministering in social space is different. In smaller groups of ten to fifteen people, we share safe snapshots of ourselves in order to assess with whom we have something in common. When we identify those with similar interests and passions, we may choose to cultivate more personal relationships with them.

Connecting in personal space occurs when we are willing to share our "private—although not 'naked'—experiences, feelings, and thoughts."[3] When you think of your important connections among a small circle of good friends (three to five people), you are thinking of personal space.

Finally, there is intimate space, representing the most vulnerable emotional expression—a space most healthy people reserve for few people other than our spouses. As Myers describes here, and as we have discussed in earlier chapters, this is relational sharing that is naked and not ashamed—the goal of every marital relationship. This is also a valid space for ministry to others outside your intimate circle.

In ministry, all four spaces share the same goal: to create a sense of belonging through sharing. It is critical here to understand that no single space fosters that sense of belonging for all people. Unfortunately, our church ministry models typically suggest otherwise. The public space of the church sanctuary on Sunday morning is a staple of Christian culture, a place where we expect people to feel like they belong. We tend to view people who feel uncomfortable in large-group worship from a deficit perspective; we see them as less sincere, less committed, and less godly. It is the church's fault that we do not embrace ministry in each of the four spaces, honoring people where they feel most comfortable.

We can learn from Jesus, who seems to have intuitively grasped what contemporary social research now describes. In some instances, Jesus ministered to large numbers of people in the synagogue as he read from the Torah or when he preached to the thousands (public space). Sometimes, he spoke parables to a small group (social space). In other instances, Jesus invested ministry seeds in even smaller groups of followers (personal space). In still other situations, Jesus ministered words of deliverance to one or two individuals (intimate space).

There is no single space that ministers to everyone. Consider how you and your spouse might minister in various spaces. In public space, you can advocate for public policies that strengthen the institution of marriage; help develop marriage enrichment programs at your church; conduct workshops in parent education, marriage enrichment, or divorce recovery; or develop materials that support marriage, such as websites, devotionals, and books. Or, you could minister in a way that has nothing to do directly with marriage.

In social space, you can either host or participate in small-group marriage-enrichment studies (e.g., *Marriage ROCKS* groups) or organize social events for premarried or married couples. In personal space, you may serve as marriage mentors and counselors or provide childcare for couples to facilitate date nights. As for intimate space, pray that God would bring you one or two couples with whom you can share the joys and challenges of marriage while holding one another accountable for growth.

Do not feel limited by these ideas. They are just a few suggestions to motivate your thinking about how you and your spouse can negotiate your respective passions into a ministry that is Bethel, the house of God.

Cultivate Communities of Belonging

Ultimately, *Marriage ROCKS* is about ministry. Husbands and wives are ministers to each other first, understanding each other, forgiving one another, and elevating to new levels of intimacy in their pursuit of partnership and covenant. As partners in covenant, they in turn minister to others within and outside their family— ministry that needs to happen wherever they find themselves—in public, social, personal, and intimate spaces.

In can be difficult for us to see our couple-selves as ministers. We recognize the pastor, the leaders of the marriage-enrichment ministry, and perhaps members of the church's counseling ministry as responsible for ministering to marriages. However, this limited perspective is not God's way. God desires to open your spiritual eyes to a world in which your marriage is a living temple, ushering the sacred into one or more of these spaces of relational belonging.

Know thyself. In which of these spaces—public, social, personal, or intimate—do you prefer interpersonal interaction? Your testimonies will resonate in some spaces and with some people more than with others. God commands us to spread knowledge of his mighty works but allows us great freedom to identify the forum we find most effective and comfortable.

You do not need to have all of the answers. As a wounded healer, your job is to tell your story of God as Deliverer, Way-maker, and Provider in your life and in your marriage. This testimony creates sacred space, a memorial to the Lord that promises to influence the lives of others for God's glory. Sacred spaces are communities that cultivate belonging—something for which postmodern culture longs. People are not always looking for commitment, but they always look for connection. The desire for connection is wired into the fabric of what it means to be human.

People are not always looking for commitment, but they always look for connection.

From Pillow to Pillar

Many couples are blind to the grace that is theirs for the claiming. We remain oblivious to the wonders that God enacts on our behalf. Graces and wonders take many forms in marriage, from the mundane to the miraculous. Only by raising your spiritual antennae can you capture God's signal and tune in. It took a place of discomfort for Jacob to catch on. For many marriages, it will take this as well.

Jacob was astonished that God was present in the very place where he lay, and believed that this place must be the gateway to heaven. Similarly, when God is speaking to you in your marriage, you must respond specifically. It is not sufficient to ponder theories of marital fulfillment or to lament the general state of marriage today. God wants your specific marriage to be the gateway to heaven for you and others with whom you come in contact.

Your marriage is the gateway to heaven because it is the instrument through which God has extended himself to earth to challenge you to become more like him. God has designed marriage to shape us into the form that he approves, in order that we might shape our culture.

Jacob's pillar of worship signifies another transition point for Jacob. In fact, each of the ROCKS has been a point of either transition (as in the vignettes of David and Joshua) or transformation (as we saw with Gideon and Jacob). God demands the same thing from us. As we awaken to see the mighty works of God in our marriages, we must see that we are living witnesses of God's power. That we endured the rough places during the night strengthens the power of our testimony in the morning.

We must learn to rest our heads upon Christ as our Rock during the difficult storms of life. Just as he did for Jacob, God is giving us the spaces we walk in, making them sacred by his presence and boldly influencing the present and the future for his kingdom. Your marriage is the pillar upon which generations will be blessed. Ministry may be one of the most important ways we can express the oneness of husband and wife in our marriages as well as our unity in the Body of Christ.

Jesus gives us the picture and potential of this unity as he emphasizes the purpose of our oneness, "so that the world may believe that you have sent me" (John 17:20-21, NRSV). The manner in which your marriage points people to Christ is indeed the capstone of our faith and your marriage.

I ROCK Exercises

Scripture Memorization: John 17:21-22, NRSV

I ask not only on behalf of those who will believe in me through their [the disciples'] word, that they may all be one. As you, Father, are in me and I am in you, may they also be in us, so that the world may believe that you have sent me.

Contemplation

Respond to the following points of contemplation in your personal journal:

1. Four spaces—public, social, personal, and intimate—were discussed in this chapter. When thinking about ministering to others, which space feels most comfortable for you individually? Which space is optimal for your ministry as a couple?

2. What does it mean to you to be planning ministry ventures with your spouse? How has this planning process been for you? In what ways could it be better?

Integration

3. Write your final letter to your spouse describing what it has meant for you to complete this *Marriage ROCKS* journey together.

We ROCK Exercises

Contemplation

1. Discuss as a couple your responses to the I ROCK Exercises. If there are ways that you could better execute this ministry planning process, take time to discuss them.
2. Considering the spaces in which you each are most comfortable, brainstorm ideas for how to execute your chosen areas of ministry. In what ways can your respective personalities be optimized for this shared ministry?

Integration

3. One key to becoming more intentional in your ministry as a couple is to operate within your respective personality structures. Take a personality assessment, such as the Primary Colors Personality Tool (available free online at http://www.dawnbillings .com) or even the Myers-Briggs (a version is available online at http://www.personalitypathways.com) to see how you can leverage your personality similarities and differences for your ministry. These assessments can also be ordered if you prefer to complete a printed version.
4. Based on your gifts, personalities, and preferred ministry spaces, write an agreement that details your plans for ministry as a couple. Remember that these ministry plans may need adjusting as you advance through the various seasons of your married life. When completed, sign your agreement. Ask your pastor to pray and anoint you and your spouse as you commit to planning and executing your ministry plan.

The Greatest Love Story

Grow old along with me.
The best is yet to be—the last of life
for which the first was made.
—Robert Browning

BIBLICAL VIGNETTE:
David's final words

Now these are the last words of David: The oracle of David, son of Jesse, the oracle of the man whom God exalted, the anointed of the God of Jacob, the favorite of the Strong One of Israel:

The Spirit of the Lord speaks through me, his word is upon my tongue. The God of Israel has spoken, the Rock of Israel has said to me: One who rules over people justly, ruling in the fear of God, is like the light of morning, like the sun rising on a cloudless morning, gleaming from the rain on the grassy land. Is not my house like this with God? For he has made with me an everlasting covenant, ordered in all things and secure. Will he not cause to prosper all my help and my desire? (2 Samuel 23:1-5, NRSV).

The New York Public Library lists Emily Brontë's *Wuthering Heights* as the greatest love story of all time. Brontë's classic is followed by Leo Tolstoy's *Anna Karenina*, with William Shakespeare's *Romeo and Juliet* rounding out the top three.[1] It is noteworthy that these three great love stories are all doomed affairs, ending with the tragic deaths of one or both lovers; certainly there is no "happily ever after" in them. Perhaps that is why these fictional depictions of love pale in comparison to the greatest love story of all time: Christ the Bridegroom's sacrifice of his life for his bride, the church. Christ's death for the sins of humanity provides a path to reunite each of us with God. But, the love story does not end here. God concerns himself with shaping us into vessels of purpose for the duration of our sojourn on earth.

We began this book with a question: Why marriage? Marriage requires that we deal with the pressures of accommodating the needs of another over our own. Marriage means that we risk exposing our deepest emotions to someone who may abuse them. In the great love stories of *Wuthering Heights* and *Anna Karenina*, the abuse and lovelessness the heroines experience in marriage is as defining as the love affairs they believe will save them. Many spouses feel vulnerable, isolated, and rudderless as they live with internal fears or an unresponsive spouse. Emotional brokenness may have created a chasm between you and your spouse that feels as wide as the Grand Canyon itself. If this describes your marriage, then the question of why marriage is a difficult one to answer.

Regardless of the state of your marriage, I am assured of one thing: Christ promises to bridge any chasm if you and your spouse choose to allow him to do so. Ultimately, it is your faith, not formulas or frameworks, that holds the answer to the marriage question. The marriage question, at its core, connects directly to the greatest love story, to your faith in the message of Jesus Christ. Christ opens your heart to experience your marriage, especially in its disappointments, as redemptive. Your personal acceptance of Christ's sacrifice on Calvary challenges you to offer first fruits to your spouse. Your belief that the Holy Spirit empowers you uniquely as a vessel of value encourages healthy boundaries. Each of these facets is enhanced as you and your partner strive to be what the apostle Peter dubbed "living stones" (1 Peter 2:5) in turning hearts toward the Lord—the Great Commission. Ultimately, the answer to the marriage question is captured in a single idea: ministry. This ministry, however, always begins at home.

Your Marriage, God's Ministry

Your marriage is designed to be part of your greatest love story, because it is about God's work on earth—God's ministry, as it were. The aim of *Marriage ROCKS* is impossible as a human endeavor. Like Jesus' exaggerated reference to a camel going through the eye of a needle (Matthew 19:24), marriage is simply too difficult, unless it is God's ministry.

A former seminary professor of mine, theologian Ray Anderson, writes, "It is God's ministry that expounds God's nature and purpose. In obedience and response to God's ministry, we gain knowledge of God and of ourselves."[2] Applied to the ministry of marriage, this means that your marriage informs your theology, or who you believe God to be. Your obedience to God's call opens your mind and heart to a personal experience of God that is without parallel. As you and your spouse see God more clearly, your purposes as individuals and as a couple are clarified. Couples who have difficulty grasping their purpose as partners in marriage may be struggling because they have not responded as partners to God's call to ministry.

Anderson goes on to say, "Whether we realize it or not, every act of ministry reveals something of God."[3] Redemption, offering, and covenant in marriage are all God's ministry working through us, revealing God's forgiveness, intimacy, and spiritual identity. In contrast to believing that our understanding of God enlightens our ministry, Anderson's position highlights that it is, in fact, ministry that enlightens who God is to you.

Marriage as ministry satisfies one's deepest longings for emotional safety, relational connection, and purpose, because it reveals God's nature (through Christ) as the embodiment of restoration, unconditional commitment, and spiritual discovery. Your marriage can leverage your attachment with your spouse to foster attachments with others. The quality of your marital attachment is intended to spark a yearning toward serving others that transcends your own self-interests. In a real sense, your obedient marriage may be the most dramatic revelation of God that some members of your family, your church, your friends, and your community will ever witness. What does your marriage reveal about God's nature?

Getting Your House Right

As we close, I find it fitting to lean once more on the words of King David in 2 Samuel 23, written as he neared the end of his life. David's words paint an idyllic portrait of God's nature as revealed through David's journey from shepherd to giant slayer to revered king, despite David's own sinfulness. In the midst of his shortcomings, David modeled righteousness and fear of God to Israel and to the world. David's righteous kingship was his ministry—one that endeared him as a man after God's own heart. Ultimately, David became confident on four fronts: that his house was right with God, that his covenant was secure, that his salvation was assured, and that God would grant the desires of his heart.

God calls you and your spouse to rule your house, like David, with righteousness and fear of God. Your marriage is your path to discovering God's nature as well as your own. David's four confidences are yours when you commit to the *Marriage ROCKS* climb. God will make your house right; his covenant promise to you as the spiritual seed of Abraham is secure. God has prepared a heavenly kingdom that awaits you, and he promises to grant the desires of your heart.

So, why marriage? None of the hundreds of books on marriage (including this one) hold the answer for you, for they are, at best, only guideposts along your journey. For me, the answer is simply about ministry. I choose marriage because I am convinced that my wife, Dalia, is God's gift to shape me into the person God purposes for me to become. I serve the same complementary role for her. Our joint demonstration of forgiveness toward each other when we err allows us to experience God as our Redeemer (1 Peter 1:17-19). Our times of prayer and intimacy reveal God as our Nurturer (Isaiah 66:13). As we struggle to negotiate conflicts in ways that honor God and each other, we understand God as Mediator (1 Timothy 2:5). Our testimonies of God's everyday miracles esteem God as the consummate Provider (Philippians

4:19). And, our resolve to sanctify our marriage as a center for worship reveres God as the Holy of Holies (Hebrews 10:19-22). Our marriage is God's ministry revealing the divine nature to us.

As I learn more of God, I fall more in love with Dalia. Like David, we revel in the confidence that our house is right with God and that God continues to honor the desires of our hearts.

As Dalia and I climb these *Marriage ROCKS*, we have one additional confidence—that the New York Public Library got it wrong. The greatest love story was not penned by Brontë over 160 years ago; rather, it is recorded in the Holy Bible—the gospel story of God's gift of the Living Word, Jesus Christ, more than two thousand years ago. However, the true beauty of this love story is that more chapters continue to be written every day by you and me as we discover authentic meaning in our marriages. Your marriage, when offered as God's ministry, continues this love story until that time when the Lord calls us all home to rest. May God richly bless you and yours. Amen.

Notes

Chapter 1: Marriage Is for God's People

1. Black Marriage Day, founded by Nisa Muhammad of the Wedded Bliss Foundation, is an annual celebration of African American marriages on the fourth Sunday of March. You can find more information on this important event at http://www.blackmarriageday.com.
2. Pew Forum on Religion & Public Life. *U.S. Religious Landscape Survey: Religious Affiliation Diverse & Dynamic.* 2008, 155.
3. Barna Group. "Ethnic Groups Differ Substantially on Matters of Faith," August 10, 2004. http://www.barna.org/barna-update/article/5-barna-update/193-ethnic-groups-differ-substantially-on-matters-of-faith (accessed March 5, 2009).

Chapter 3: Relinquishing Your Imaginary Marriage

1. Harville Hendrix. *Getting the Love You Want: A Guide for Couples.* (New York: Harper, 1988), 8.
2. Deborah Tannen. *You Just don't Understand: Women and Men in Conversation.* (New York: William Morrow and Company, 1990), 23–48.

Chapter 6: Step 3: Present An Acceptable Offering

1. Shmuel Silinsky. "Understanding the Sacrifices," January 26, 2000. http://www.aish.com/literacy/judaism123/Understanding_the_Sacrifices.asp (accessed April 6, 2009).

Chapter 8: Step 5: Make TIME for Intimacy

1. Willard F. Harley Jr. *His Needs Her Needs: Building an Affair-proof Marriage.* (Grand Rapids, MI: Fleming H. Revell, 1994), 12–13.
2. Gary Rosberg and Barbara Rosberg. *The 5 Love Needs of Men & Women.* (Wheaton, IL: Tyndale, 2000), 8.

3. Roger Dobson. "How the power of touch reduces pain and even fights disease," October 10, 2006. http://www.independent.co.uk/life-style/health-and-wellbeing/health-news/how-the-power-of-touch-reduces-pain-and-even-fights-disease-419462.html (accessed April 6, 2009).

4. Dobson.

5. James Coan, Hillary Schaefer, and Richard Davidson. "Lending a Hand: Social Regulation of the Neural Response to Threat," *Psychological Science* 17 (12) (2006): 1032–1039.

6. Matthew Hertensetin. Dacher Keltner, Betsy App, Brittany A. Bulleit, and Ariane R. Jaskolka "Touch Communicates Distinct Emotions." *Emotion* 6 (3) (2006): 528–533.

7. Jack O. Balswick and Judy K. Balswick. *The Family: A Christian Perspective on the Contemporary Home.* (Grand Rapids, MI: Baker, 1991), 87.

8. Rosberg and Rosberg, 8.

Chapter 9: Step 6: Check the Boundaries of Your Marriage

1. Henry Cloud, John Townsend. *Boundaries: When to Say Yes, When to Say No To Take Control of Your Life.* (Grand Rapids, MI: Zondervan, 1992), 239–268.

Chapter 10: Step 7: Keep Covenant in Your Conflict

1. John M. Gottman. *The Seven Principles for Making Marriage Work.* (New York: Random House, 1999), 129–155.

Chapter 13: Step 10: Mobilize Your Marriage for Worship

1. Barna Group, 1.

Chapter 15: Step 12: Cultivate Communities of Belonging

1. Edward Hall. *The Hidden Dimension: Man's Use of Space in Public and Private.* (Garden City, NY: Doubleday/Anchor Books, 1966)

2. Joseph Myers. *The Search to Belong: Rethinking Intimacy, Community, and Small Groups.* (Grand Rapids, MI: Zondervan, 2003), 41.

3. Myers, 47.

Epilogue: The Greatest Love Story

1. Reuters Life. "Classic tales top list of greatest love stories," April 11, 2007. http://www.reuters.com/article/gc08/idUSN1041895020070411 (accessed August 29, 2009).

2. Ray Anderson. *The Soul of Ministry: Forming Leaders for God's People.* (Louisville: Westminister John Knox Press, 1997), 3.

3. Anderson, 7.